In Step with the Spirit

In Step with the Spirit

Discovering the Dynamics
of the Deeper Life

A.B. Simpson

CHRISTIAN PUBLICATIONS
CAMP HILL, PENNSYLVANIA

Christian Publications
3825 Hartzdale Drive
Camp Hill, PA 17011
www.cpi-horizon.com

Faithful, biblical publishing since 1883

ISBN: 0-87509-660-3
LOC Catalog Card Number: 96-83382

98 99 00 01 02   5 4 3 2 1

Formerly published under the titles
Walking in the Spirit
and
The Gentle Love of the Holy Spirit.

CONTENTS

1 Living in the Spirit 1

2 Walking in the Spirit 9

3 Person and Attributes
   of the Holy Spirit 19

4 Offices and Relations
   of the Holy Spirit 25

5 The Spirit of Light 33

6 The Spirit of Holiness 53

7 The Spirit of Life 69

8 The Spirit of Comfort 85

9 The Spirit of Love 99

10 The Spirit of Power 113

11 The Spirit of Prayer 139

12 Cooperating with the Holy Spirit 151

13 Hindering the Holy Spirit 163

Living in the Spirit

Since we live by the Spirit, let us keep in step with the Spirit. (Galatians 5:25)

To live in the Spirit is to be born of the Spirit. It is to have received a new spiritual life from above. "Flesh gives birth to flesh, but the Spirit gives birth to spirit" (John 3:6). "Jesus answered, 'I tell you the truth, no one can enter the kingdom of God unless he is born of water and the Spirit'" (3:5). "Therefore, if anyone is in Christ, he is a new creation; the old has gone, the new has come!" (2 Corinthians 5:17).

We may have the brightest intellectual life, the most unblemished moral character and the most amiable qualities of disposition. Yet without the new life of the Holy Spirit in our heart, we can no more enter heaven than the lovely canary that sings in our window can become a member of our

family, or the gentle lamb that our children play
with can sit down at our table and share our do-
mestic fellowship and enjoyment. They belong to
a different world, and nothing but a new nature
and human heart could bring them into fellowship
with our human life. The most exalted intellect
and the most attractive, natural disposition reach
no higher than the earthly. The kingdom of
heaven consists of the family of God—those who
have risen to an entirely different sphere, having
received a nature as much above the intellectual
and moral as God (1 John 3:1)!

A modern writer has expressed this thought of
the difference between the various orders of life,
even in the natural world. The little tuft of moss
that grows upon the granite rock can look down
from immeasurable heights upon the mass of
stone on which it rests and say, "I am transcendently above you, for I have life, vegetable life,
and you are inorganic mass!" And yet, as we ascend one step, the smallest insect that crawls upon
the majestic palm tree can look down upon the
most beautiful production of the vegetable world
and say, "I am transcendently above you, for I
have animal life, and you are not even conscious of
your own loveliness, or of the little creature that
feeds upon your blossom!"

Still higher we ascend, until we reach the world
of mind. The youngest child of the most illiterate
peasant can say to the mightiest creations of the
animal world—to the majestic lion, king of the forest, the soaring eagle of the skies, the many-tinted

bird of paradise or the noble steed that bears his master like the whirlwind over the desert—"I am your lord, for I possess intellectual life. You have neither soul nor reason, and must perish with your expiring breath and become like the clods beneath your feet, but I shall live forever."

But there is still another step beyond all this. There is a spiritual world which is as much higher than the intellectual as that is above the physical; the humblest and most uncultured Christian, who has just learned to pray and say, "Our Father in heaven" (Matthew 6:9) from the depths of a regenerate heart is as much above the loftiest genius of the world of mind as he is above the material creation at his feet.

This is the meaning of Christianity: It is the breath of a new nature; it is the translation of the soul into a higher universe and a loftier scale of being, even introducing it into the family of God Himself and making it a partaker of the divine nature. This is indeed a stupendous mystery and an endowment whose glory may well fill our hearts with everlasting wonder as we cry with the adoring apostle, "How great is the love the Father has lavished on us, that we should be called children of God!" (1 John 3:1).

Not merely by adoption are we admitted to the Father's house, but by actual birth. From the very bosom of the Holy Spirit, as from a heavenly mother, has our new spirit been born—just as literally as Jesus Christ Himself was born of the eternal Spirit in the bosom of Mary. So it might be said of every newborn soul: "The Holy Spirit will come upon you, and the power of the Most High will overshadow you. So the holy one to be born will be called the Son of God" (Luke 1:35). Beloved, do we thus live in the Spirit? This is everlasting life.

To live in the Spirit is also to be baptized of the Holy Spirit and to have the Spirit as a divine Person living in us. There is something higher than the new birth, namely, the entering in of the Comforter in His personal fullness and glory to dwell in the consecrated heart and abide there forever.

Jesus was born of the Spirit in Bethlehem, but He was baptized of the Spirit 30 years later on the banks of the Jordan. This made all the difference which we trace between His quiet years at Nazareth and His public ministry in Galilee and Judea. From that time there were two persons united in the ministry of Jesus of Nazareth. The Holy Spirit, as a divine Person, was united with the Person of Jesus Christ and was the source of His power and the inspiration of His teaching. He constantly represented Himself as speaking the words and doing the works which the Spirit in Him prompted.

And so there is in the believer's life a similar experience, when the soul truly converted to God yields itself wholly to His control and becomes the living temple of the Almighty Spirit. From that time forward this Spirit dwells in it and walks in it, giving it not only a new nature, which it received in regeneration, but Himself, a divine

Guest, a Presence, to dwell in that new nature as its controlling guide and almighty strength.

Then is fulfilled the double promise of Ezekiel: "I will give you a new heart and put a new spirit in you; . . . And I will put my Spirit in you and move you to follow my decrees and be careful to keep my laws" (36:26-27). From now on, we live in the Spirit in a higher sense than even after our conversion. Our life is not only spiritual but divine. Now it is not we who live, but Christ who lives in us. We draw from Him, through the Holy Spirit, every moment, life and health, joy and peace.

It is not living *through* the Spirit, but living *in* the Spirit. He is the very element of our new existence: before us, behind us, above us, beneath us, within us, beyond us. We are buried in Him, lost in Him, encompassed by Him as by the air we breathe. This is the yet higher mystery of the new life, greater than the new birth. This is the secret which Paul declares was hid for ages and generations, but is now made manifest to His saints—"Christ in you, the hope of glory" (Colossians 1:27).

It is indeed an epoch in the soul's existence as wonderful in its measure as when the Son of God became incarnate on earth, when the Holy One crosses the threshold of the heart, makes the spirit His personal residence, sits down upon the throne of the human will and assumes the government and control of all our being and destiny. We may indeed walk with holy veneration and exalted hope, exultant in joy and triumph as wondering angels declare, "Now the dwelling of God is with men, and he will live with them. They will be his people, and God himself will be with them and be their God" (Revelation 21:3).

Have you claimed this high privilege and received this heavenly Guest into your regenerated soul? Have you received the invaluable jewel of the Living One Himself, as the treasure in the earthen vessel and the glory in the midst?

To live in the Spirit is to be sanctified by the Spirit, to receive the Spirit of holiness and thus be delivered from the power of sin. They who receive the Holy Spirit can say, "[B]ecause through Christ Jesus the law of the Spirit of life set me free from the law of sin and death" (Romans 8:2). This is divine holiness; it is the entrance into a sinful heart of a new life which excludes the old and takes its place. It is not the cleansing of the flesh or the improving of the life of self; rather, it is the imparting to us of a new life which is in itself essentially pure and cannot sin, even the holy life of God.

In our childhood many of us have roamed through the native woods and seen some old, fallen forest tree rotting where it lay. Through the decaying wood the earthworms and insects burrow, and perhaps some poisonous snake has built its nest and raised its brood, so that we have feared to sit down on the old, putrefying mass and have thought of it as a type of corruption and decay.

That mass of putrefaction may well represent the ruin of our old sinful nature. But have we not sometimes seen a little shoot of unsullied whiteness in the early spring growing up through the rotten wood—rising out of the mass of corruption as the beautiful and pure hand of a baby, unstained even by the touch of the corrupting element around it—until it has grown into a tree from whose branches have been plucked the luscious fruit of the summer woods? It was life in the midst of death, purity amid corruption, having no connection whatever with the soil in which it grew and incapable of mixing with its defilement.

Precisely so is the life of holiness in the soul. Like that stainless shoot, it grew from a divine root and has nothing in common with our own sinful nature. It is of heavenly origin, and it grows up within us in its own divine purity and fruitfulness until it ripens into all the rich fruition of a consecrated and heavenly life. Yet at every stage we feel that it is in no sense our own life, but the indwelling presence and purity of God Himself.

Have we received this sanctifying Spirit and learned this heavenly secret of holy living? And in all the exquisite rest and conscious purity and overcoming power of His presence, have we learned to live in the Spirit?

To live in the Spirit is to receive the quickening life of the Holy Spirit in our physical being and to find in Him the source of constant stimulus and strength for all the faculties of our mind and all the functions of our body. "And if the Spirit of him who raised Jesus from the dead is living in you, he who raised Christ from the dead will also give life to your mortal bodies through his Spirit, who lives in you" (Romans 8:11).

The subtle principle of life itself came originally, no doubt, from His inbreathing at man's creation. Then why should it be thought anything incredible that He should still breathe upon our flesh the quickening life of the ascended Son of God? Are we not members of His body, His flesh and His bones? And does He not speak of a distinct sense in which our body is the temple of the Holy Spirit? Indeed it was the Holy Spirit who, during Christ's ministry, always gave efficiency to His healing word. He is still the same infinite and inexhaustible life, and the bodies of His consecrated people are the subject of His divine influence and of His sustaining love and care.

Have we learned the secret of His strength? Like Samson, do we know what it is to be moved by the Spirit until the earthen vessel becomes mighty through God to do and endure where earthly strength must fail? They who thus "hope in the LORD will renew their strength. They will soar on wings like eagles; they will run and not grow weary, they will walk and not be faint" (Isaiah 40:31).

Walking in the Spirit

*Since we live by the Spirit, let us keep in step
with the Spirit. (Galatians 5:25)*

What is it to walk in the Spirit? Generally, it
may be said, it is to maintain the habit of
dependence upon the Holy Spirit for our entire
life—spirit, soul and body. We know what it is at
times to enjoy His conscious presence. We live in
the Spirit and we have felt the touch of His quickening life. Now let us walk in the Spirit. Let us
abide in this fellowship. Let us lean continually
upon His strength and drink unceasingly from
His life.

If we would walk in the Spirit we must recognize the Spirit as present and abiding in us. How
often, after we have asked for His presence, we
treat Him as if He had deceived us and cry to
Him as if He were far off? Let us recognize Him

as having come and address Him as a present and indwelling friend. He will always respond to our recognition and speak to us as the ancient presence—not from the mount or the pillar of fire, but from the tabernacle and from the holy of holies in our inmost heart.

If we would walk in the Spirit we must trust Him and count upon Him in the emergencies of life. We must regard Him as one who has undertaken our cause and expects to be called upon in every time of need, one who will unfailingly be found faithful and all-sufficient in every crisis. The very name Paraclete means one that we can always call upon and find at our side. We must trust the Holy Spirit and expect Him to respond to our need implicitly, as we expect the air to answer the opening of our lungs and the sunrise to meet us in the morning. And yet how many treat the Holy Spirit as if He were a capricious and most unreliable friend! How many of our prayers are despairing groans or scolding reflections on His love and faithfulness!

It was for this that Moses lost the Promised Land. Instead of quietly speaking to the rock and expecting its waters to flow forth to meet his call, he struck it with hasty and unbelieving violence and spoke as one who did not fully trust the love and faithfulness of God. There is no need that we should strike the rock or cry, like Baal's priests, to the distant heavens for help. Let us gently and implicitly claim the love that is always in advance even of our prayer. Let us speak in the whisper of childlike trust to that heart which is ever ready to pour its fullness into our emptiness. Then the waters will gush forth, and the desert of our sorrows, doubts and fears will blossom as the rose.

3)   If we would walk in the Spirit we must continually consult the Spirit. We shall often find that the things that seem easiest will fail and disappoint us when we rely upon their apparent probability and the mere promise of outward circumstances. We shall also find that when we commit our way unto Him and acknowledge Him in all our ways, He will so direct our paths that the things which seemed most difficult and improbable will become the easiest and most successful. He desires to teach us to trust Him with all our heart, and lean not unto our own understanding; in all our ways to acknowledge Him and He will direct our steps (Proverbs 3:5-6).

   The chief condition of His almighty power is that we shall first have His omniscient wisdom. He is given to us as our wonderful Counselor and also as our mighty God. I have never taken Him as my Counselor and obeyed His guidance without finding that He followed it up as the Mighty One with His omnipotent working. The reason we do not more frequently find His power is because we try to turn it into the channels of our own wisdom instead of getting His mind, working in His will and even knowing that we must have His effectual working. How blessed that His guidance offered to each of us is as simple, as accessible as the hand of a child!

So let us walk in the Spirit, trusting His guiding hand and committing all our ways to His wisdom and love.

4) If we would walk in the Spirit we must obey Him when He speaks. We must remember that the first part of obedience is to listen. It is not enough to say we have done all we know. We ought to know, and we may know, for He has said that we shall know His voice. If we do not, it must be that we are to blame, or else God is responsible for our mistake. But this cannot be!

If we will be still, suppress our own impulses and clamorous desires and meet Him with a heart surrendered to His will and guidance, we shall know His way. "He guides the humble in what is right and teaches them his way" (Psalm 25:9). The soul that walks in the Spirit will therefore be an attentive spirit, watching daily at His doors and longing to know His very commandments. When we understand His voice we will implicitly obey it. Obedience to the Spirit is life and peace. The very condition of His continual presence is obedience: "the Holy Spirit, whom God has given to those who obey him" (Acts 5:32).

The secret of every cloud that has fallen upon the soul will probably be found in some neglected voice of our Monitor. He is waiting and has been waiting for us at that point where we have refused to follow, and when we step into His will we shall find Him there.

5) If we would walk in the Spirit we must keep

step with the Holy Spirit. Our obedience should be so prompt that we shall never find ourselves a step behind Him or following Him at a distance which we may find it hard to regain.

On our great railroads there are certain trains which run upon the highest possible schedule of time. The itinerary is so arranged that there is no margin allowed on which to overtake lost time, so that should the train be late it is nearly impossible to regain the interval lost. God has drawn the plan of our life on such a scale that there are no minutes left blank, and if we lose one the next has no margin to afford for its recovery. All that we can crowd into the future will be needed for the future itself, and therefore if we lose a step there is danger that we shall continue to be a step behind. It will then require the same exertion to keep even a step behind as it would to walk abreast of God every moment.

A millrace needs just as much water to run at low as at high tide. The very same quantity of water, if kept up to the level of the wheel, will run all the ponderous machinery as that which on a lower level only wastes itself in fretting wavelets among the rocks of the torrent bed. And so it is just as easy for our spiritual life to move at the maximum as at the minimum, if we only start at the right level and guard the moments so that we shall not lose our headway or get behind God.

The secret of this one blessing is instant obedience and walking moment by moment with Him in the fullness of His blessed will. Let us not disappoint Him. Let us not come short of all the good pleasure of His goodness. His thought for us is always best; His commandments "for our good always" (Deuteronomy 6:24, KJV); His schedule of our life's journey planned by unerring wisdom and unutterable love.

He has given us a gentle, patient Guide who is willing to go with us all the way and come into even the smallest steps of our life. Let us take heed that we do not grieve Him away or miss anything of His gentle will. Let us be sensitive to His touch, responsive to His whisper, obedient to His commandments, and ever able to say, "The one who sent me is with me; he has not left me alone, for I always do what pleases him" (John 8:29).

The Blessings of Walking in the Spirit

Such a walk will secure for us a complete and delightful deliverance from sin. The expulsive power of His presence will drive out the presence of evil. "So I say, live by the Spirit, and you will not gratify the desires of the sinful nature" (Galatians 5:16). In this way our life shall be transformed from a defensive warfare, in which we are always attacking evil, to a glorious consciousness of God only, which shall exclude the evil from our thoughts as well as from our life. We shall not have to constantly clear the sunken rocks from our channel. Rather, on the high and full torrent of the divine life we shall rise far above every obstruction and move, as in Ezekiel's vision, in a river of life which shall be above the ankles, above the loins, a river to swim in, carrying us by its own substantial fullness.

Such a walk will give us a delightful serenity, tranquility and steadfastness to our whole life. We shall not be at the bidding of impulses or circumstances, but shall move on in the majestic order of the divine will, carried above the vicissitudes of failure and outward change, and fulfilling, like the stars in their courses, the full circle of His will for our life.

Such a walk will enable us to meet, in victory, the providences of God as they come to us, and to maintain the perfect harmony between our inward life and the outward leadings of His own. We have some beautiful examples of the transcendent importance of this walking in the Spirit in connection with the combination of circumstances on which so much often hangs.

There never was a moment in human history on which more depended than when the infant Christ was first brought into the Temple. What an honor and a privilege it was to be there and to catch the first glimpse of His blessed face, and even hold in the embrace of human arms the Gift of ages! Yet that was the honor of two aged pilgrims who were walking in the Spirit. Simeon and Anna, led of the Holy Spirit, came into the Temple at that very moment. Unerringly, and walking step by step with Him, they were enabled to meet Christ in this glorious opportunity and be among the first heralds of His coming. No wonder the aged Simeon, as he took Him in his arms, could ask no more on earth: "Sovereign Lord, as you have promised, you now dismiss your servant in peace. For my eyes have seen your salvation" (Luke 2:29-30).

Only less important was the crisis in the apostolic church when the gospel was to be preached to a new circle of disciples. The man chosen to carry the glad tidings to the Samaritans and Gentiles and to be the pioneer of Christianity among all the tribes of the heathen world, in that great progression of which the churches of Christendom today form the outcome, was a humble disciple whom God could trust to walk in the Spirit and obey the slightest intimation of His will. It was Philip, the humble deacon. Already he had been sent to Samaria to preach the gospel in that city, no doubt in obedience to a similar divine message. But in the very height of his successful work in that city, the command suddenly came to leave his work and go down to the desert of the South.

To most persons it would have seemed a misleading, a mistake, a neglect of providential duty, a waste of precious time and an arresting of the great work in Samaria. But Philip immediately obeyed. At every step of his journey he waited for new directions, and in due time the path was made plain. The first fruits of the heathen world were waiting at that very moment for his direction. And there on the crossroads of life, at the fitting moment, the Spirit brought two men together. The words which were spoken in that chariot changed the destiny of a life and the course of a dispensation, opened the gospel to the whole world and sent the Ethiopian eunuch to his home to be, in all probability, the founder of many of those mighty churches which for the next four centuries made northern Africa the most important seat of ancient Christianity.

Yet, when his work with the eunuch was accomplished, the command was distinct—to leave his new convert in the hands of the Lord and follow on at the unknown leading of the same blessed Spirit that had brought them together. "The Spirit of the Lord suddenly took Philip away, and the eunuch did not see him again" (Acts 8:39).

These are but some instances of the blessedness of this heavenly walk. Shall we trust our unseen Guide? As we step out into the mysterious and momentous future, shall we walk more humbly, simply, instantly and obediently in the companionship of His guiding hand?

CHAPTER

3

Person and Attributes of the Holy Spirit

For God did not give us a spirit of timidity, but a spirit of power, of love and of self-discipline. (2 Timothy 1:7)

The Holy Spirit is a Person, a distinct individual, and not a vague influence or a phase of divine working.

Just as there may be three judges on the bench constituting the one court, or three persons in the household constituting the one family, so there are three distinct persons in the Godhead, forming the one Deity and acting more perfectly as one in nature, volition and action than is possible for any created beings.

The Holy Spirit is constantly spoken of in the Scriptures as possessing the attributes of a person.

The personal pronoun is used to describe Him—
not *it*, but *He*! The strongest and most distinctive
of the Greek pronouns, the word *autos*, which
means "himself" and distinguishes personality as
no English term can, is often used for Him as in
First Corinthians 12:11: "All these are the work of
one and the same Spirit." Again, the attribute of
will is ascribed to Him in the same passage, "as he
determines," and there is no stronger proof of personality than the power of choice. It is the most
distinctive thing in any human being, and it is
constantly attributed to the Holy Spirit.

Again, all the emotions proper to a person are
ascribed to Him: He loves, is grieved, is provoked,
vexed, resisted and, in short, is susceptible to all
the feelings that are proper only for an intelligent
person.

The Holy Spirit Is a Divine Person

This glorious Being is no less than God. He receives the divine names. Peter told Ananias that in
lying to the Holy Spirit he had not lied to men but
to God. Christ declared that in casting out devils by
the Holy Spirit, He did it by the finger of God.

He possesses divine attributes. He is omniscient: "The Spirit searches all things" (1 Corinthians 2:10). He is omnipresent: "Where can I go
from your Spirit? Where can I flee from your
presence?" (Psalm 139:7) He is omnipotent; for
Christ declares, "What is impossible with men
[namely, the salvation of the human soul] is possible with God" (Luke 18:27). It is the Holy Spirit

that converts the soul; therefore, He must have the omnipotence of God.

He is called the Holy Spirit, and holiness is a divine attribute. Again, He performs the works of God; He was a partaker in the work of creation— the Spirit of light, order, beauty and life. He accomplishes the regeneration and sanctification of the soul, which are divine works. He effected the incarnation and resurrection of the Son of God, and He will participate in the final resurrection of the saints of God from the grave at the Lord's coming. Such works could be performed by no man, and they stamp Him as divine.

Finally, He receives divine worship; His name is associated with the Father and the Son in apostolic benediction, the formula of baptism and the worship of the heavenly host. And John opens the Apocalypse with an ascription of praise which links Him with the Father and would be blasphemy if He were not God.

The Personal Attributes of the Holy Spirit

He is "a spirit of power, of love and of self-discipline" (2 Timothy 1:7).

The Holy Spirit has power: He is almighty. Within the sphere of His special office and operations there is nothing He cannot do; there is no case too hard for His working, no soul too lost for Him to save, too hard for Him to soften, too vile for Him to sanctify or too weak for Him to use.

He is the Spirit of creation. Look out upon the springing forces of nature, throbbing in the springtime of life and glory. How quietly, majestically and resistlessly nature is moving on to the resurrection of the year, to the fullness and glory of the summer and the harvest. How abundant the exuberant life and power we behold on every hand! It covers the forest and the field with a profusion of flowers, foliage and fruitfulness beyond the actual needs of earth's inhabitants, scattering with tropical bounty the gifts of God, as though His strength and love were so full He knew not how to find vent for all its overflow.

Why should He be less full, less bountiful, less almighty in the realm of grace? On the contrary, larger and nobler still is His promise here. "For I will pour water on the thirsty land, and streams on the dry ground" (Isaiah 44:3) is His marvelous promise.

There is no stint to His resources. Let us enter into His omnipotence and go forth, knowing the might of our God and claiming the full plentitude of His power and grace.

But mightier still is the power displayed in the resurrection of Jesus Christ. When the apostle would lift our conception up to an adequate realization of the hope of our calling, the riches of the glory of our inheritance and the exceeding greatness of God's power to us who believe, he points us to that transcendent miracle, the resurrection of Jesus Christ. He sees Him, without an effort, bursting the bonds of death, snapping asunder the sealed tomb, rising up above all the power of death and the natural law of mortality, above the laws of the material world. He pictures Him passing through the closed door and rising above the solid earth as He triumphantly ascends above all might and dominion, far above all principality and power, higher and higher till He is above the earth, above the sky, above the heavens, above every name that is named, not only in this world but that which is to come.

And then He sees us seated by His side and raised up by the same Holy Spirit to share in all the fullness of Christ's ascension, glory and power. This is the measure of the power of grace. Let us claim it in all its majestic fullness and bring it down to lift up our life and the souls around us to the heights of grace and glory.

The Holy Spirit is love: His love is even greater than His power. All the terms in which He is described are notes of tenderness and expressions of gentleness, loveliness and grace. "I urge you, . . ." says Paul, "by the love of the Spirit" (Romans 15:30). What love it was for Jesus Christ to live for 30 years and more in this uncongenial world. The Holy Spirit loves not less, for He has lived for thousands of years in this scene of sin and this land of enemies.

How gentle the love of Jesus is, coming so near to sinful men. But the Holy Spirit has come still nearer; He enters our very hearts and dwells in the inmost being of lost and worthless men.

How marvelous the grace of Christ that endured the shame and spitting, the rejection and

crucifixion of the judgment hall and the cross! But
not less marvelous is the gentleness which has
pleaded for ages with wicked men, borne all their
resistance, rebellion and rejection and yet waited
through a whole lifetime to win the faintest response from their faith or love.

How much He has borne from each of us; how
gently and patiently He has suffered our slights,
endured our ignorance, stupidity, gross and direct
disobedience!

How close He is willing to come to the heart;
how unreserved and condescending His intimacy
and affection; how dear we are to Him! None but
His loved ones know how exquisite and intimate
the communion which we may enjoy under His
wings and on the bosom of His love. We may tell
Him all our sorrow and care and find Him responsive to every whisper and breathing of our
heart—ever near, by day or by night. He is our
blessed Paraclete, the ever-present One, ready to
help in every time of need.

He asks more of our trust and love; let Him not
ask in vain. Let us know, and prove, and fully appreciate the love of the Spirit.

The Holy Spirit is wisdom: He is the Spirit of
wisdom. Not only can He give us wisdom, but
with a wisdom greater than all that we may see
He is guiding, teaching, overruling all our life. Let
us trust His wisdom, love and power. Let us yield
ourselves with a glad "Yes!" to His every call, that
we may know the full blessing of "walking in the
Spirit."

Offices and Relations
of the Holy Spirit

There are different kinds of gifts, but the same
Spirit. There are different kinds of service, but
the same Lord. There are different kinds of
working, but the same God works all of them in
all men. (1 Corinthians 12:4-6)

The Holy Spirit has a special place in the divine economy.

With respect to the Father, He is spoken of as
proceeding from Him; the same term is also used
of His relation to the Son. He has been called the
executive of the Godhead.

Many figures have been used, although all such
figures must ever be unsatisfactory, to illustrate
the relation of the divine Persons. Perhaps the
most successful is that which compares them to

the various forms of light. Thus, primeval light represents the Father. Solar light, that is light centered in an actual sun, represents the Son. Atmospheric light, that is the light reflected and refracted and turned into vision and illumination in the atmosphere and the world around us, represents the Holy Spirit, who brings us the divine Presence and practically applies to us the benefits of God's revelation and grace.

His relation to the Second Person of the Godhead is very clearly revealed; it was He who ministered in His incarnation and through whom He became the Son of Man as well as the Son of God. It was He who personally united Himself with the person of Christ and became the power of all His miracles and teachings. It was He through whom he "offered himself unblemished to God" (Hebrews 9:14). It was He through whom He arose from the dead. And after His resurrection it was by the Holy Spirit that He gave commandment to His apostles of all things concerning the kingdom of heaven. Again, it was in His own Person that He received and shed forth the same Spirit of Pentecost upon His disciples, so that Jesus is ever identified with the Holy Spirit in all His work and ministry.

Nor is there any reason to suppose that He will be sent from the world in the millennial kingdom but will be an actual and joyful witness of the blessed fruits of His own gracious working, as well as the Savior's suffering and death.

The Relation of the Holy Spirit to the World and the Sinner

The world cannot accept Him is Christ's own explanation of His relation to the unsaved. The reason: "because it neither sees him nor knows him" (John 14:17). The Holy Spirit cannot dwell in an unconverted soul. On man's flesh the anointing oil could not be poured of old, nor can it now.

At the same time, He can and does work in the hearts of the unconverted, producing conviction and conversion and leading them to a saving union with the person of Christ.

This is His own special work. The sinful soul is dead in trespasses and sins, and it is His to quicken it, to convict of sin and then of righteousness and judgment. He brings to the heart the revelation of Jesus and, as it accepts Him, the assurance of pardon, the peace of God and all the quickened graces of the new life in Christ.

His Relation to the Believer

Having led the soul to Christ, the Holy Spirit now becomes the personal Guide, Teacher, Sanctifier and Comforter of the believer. His various ministries will be unfolded in the following chapters.

When the heart is fully surrendered to Him, He becomes its personal, permanent, indwelling Guest. He brings with Him the manifested presence of the Father and the Son. He leads the believer into all truth, guides in all the will of God, supplies all the needed grace, unfolds the life of Jesus Christ in his life and develops in him all the fruit of the Spirit in their full variety and complete maturity.

He is the Spirit of light and revelation, of guidance and of wisdom. He is the Spirit of holiness. He is the Spirit of peace, joy and comfort. He is the Spirit of love, gentleness, patience, meekness and forbearance. He is the Spirit of prayer and intercession. He is the Spirit of power for service and the source of all our gifts as well as graces. He is the Spirit of physical life and healing. He is the Spirit of faith and hope, enabling us to claim the promises of God and revealing to us the glorious prospects of the future.

Our whole spiritual life is nourished and cherished by His love and care. All we are and have and may become in our Christian life is due to His personal indwelling and His faithful love and infinite grace.

But in all His work in the believer's heart and life He represents and reveals not His own person or ours, but the Lord Jesus. He is the Spirit of Christ; "he will testify about me" (John 15:26). "He will bring glory to me," was the Master's own language, "by taking from what is mine and making it known to you" (16:14).

He reveals to us our personal union with Jesus and makes Christ actual to our consciousness. "On that day," that is, when He comes, "you will realize that I am in my Father, and you are in me, and I am in you" (John 14:20).

Like the telescope, which shows the observer not its own beauty but the heavenly orbs on which we gaze, so the Holy Spirit becomes the invisible medium through whom we behold the face of Jesus and are brought into the consciousness of His grace and fellowship.

Therefore, the soul is conscious of Christ, rather than the Spirit, even in the moment of His most blessed visitations. And yet we may be directly conscious of the Spirit also. We may hold immediate fellowship with Him personally, receive the assurance of His love and pour out into His heart our gratitude and affection.

Relation to the Church

The Holy Spirit comes not only to the individual believer but to the collective body of the people of God. It is He who constitutes the Church and clothes her with the life and power of her Living Head. Until the day of Pentecost and the descent of the Spirit, the apostles were not permitted to go forth to speak and work for the Master.

The Holy Spirit is the very life and power of Christianity. Without Him the Church is like a ship without fire in her engine or steam in her boiler; like an army of soldiers lying lifeless; like Ezekiel's vision in the plain; like a body without an animated soul.

The Church was never intended to be a natural and intellectual organization, but a supernatural instrumentality wholly dependent upon the direct power of God for all her efficiency and, therefore, needing to be ever separated from the arm of flesh and the strength of mere human agencies.

The Church in which the Holy Spirit abides is no mere sectarian fragment but the whole body of believers united to Christ, the living Head. "There is one body and one Spirit—just as you were called to one hope when you were called" (Ephesians 4:4). "For we were all baptized by one Spirit into one body" (1 Corinthians 12:13).

> There are different kinds of gifts, but the same Spirit. There are different kinds of service, but the same Lord. There are different kinds of working, but the same God works all of them in all men. . . .
>
> To one there is given through the Spirit the message of wisdom, to another the message of knowledge by means of the same Spirit, to another faith by the same Spirit, to another gifts of healing by that one Spirit, to another miraculous powers, to another prophecy, to another distinguishing between spirits, to another speaking in different kinds of tongues, and to still another the interpretation of tongues. All these are the work of one and the same Spirit, and he gives them to each one, just as he determines.
>
> The body is a unit, though it is made up of many parts; and though all its parts are many, they form one body. So it is with

Christ. For we were all baptized by one Spirit into one body—whether Jews or Greeks, slave or free—and we were all given the one Spirit to drink.

Now the body is not made up of one part but of many. (1 Corinthians 12:4-6, 8-14)

The Relation of the Holy Spirit to the Various Dispensations

In all the dispensational periods of the past, the Holy Spirit has been present. Even in the antediluvian days He strove with men. Under the Levitical economy He was present, qualifying the builders of the tabernacle for their work, anointing Moses, Aaron and Joshua for their ministries, inspiring the ancient prophets for their messages and enabling the individual believers of the Old Testament to know, believe and obey God in the measure of their spiritual life.

But until after Christ's ascension the Holy Spirit was not personally resident as He is now. His influences were exercised upon the hearts of men; but His presence was not localized, as it has been since the day of Pentecost, in the body of Christ, the Church.

Since the beginning of the Christian dispensation, however, He has resided on earth and not in heaven, and is here locally as the Lord Jesus was during His earthly life. The transcendent preeminence which a New Testament saint enjoys is that his soul and body become the living and actual temple of the Holy Spirit.

This is the time of His special working. In this age we may look for His unlimited operations and anticipate toward its close the mightiest triumphs of His grace and power as He ushers in the millennial age, with the personal presence of Christ once more on earth as in the days of His flesh.

Even then the Holy Spirit will not be absent; He will ever reside in the believer and the Church.

The question has been argued whether the Holy Spirit will be present on earth during the tribulation days, after the waiting saints have been translated to be with the Lord in the air. We cannot doubt that He will still remain on earth, for how else could the Jewish remnant who shall follow the Lamb be converted, sustained and saved? And what about the Gentile remnant who during those awful days shall turn to the Lord—including perhaps many of the members of a cold church who were not ready for the Master's coming at the time of His appearing?

We cannot agree with the view of some—that when the saints are caught up to meet the Lord the Holy Spirit shall be taken away from the earth. We believe He has chosen this dark abode of sin and sorrow as the scene of His ceaseless and ultimately triumphant labors, and that He shall yet rejoice over it as a restored and renovated realm, shining in all the loveliness, sinlessness and blessedness of His accomplished restoration.

The Spirit of Light

We have not received the spirit of the world but the Spirit who is from God, that we may understand what God has freely given us. (1 Corinthians 2:12)

The first aspect in which the Holy Spirit is revealed to us is as the Illuminator and Guide of our life. Even in the story of creation, the first result of His brooding over the face of the deep is the command, "Let there be light" (Genesis 1:3). He is the Creator of the human mind and the Source of all the true light of reason and natural religion in the world; He is the true Source of spiritual light. One of His special emblems is the oil and the sevenfold lamp of the temple.

The Light of Truth

He has inspired the Holy Scriptures, the revelation of God's will and the invaluable light that shines upon the heart of man, the pathway of the unseen world. The Bible is a standard of spiritual truth, and in all His teachings and leadings the Holy Spirit never contradicts His own word. They who are more fully led of the Spirit will always most reverence the authority of the Scriptures and walk in the most perfect conformity with their principles and precepts.

But it is not enough to have the letter of the word; He who gave it must also interpret it and make it Spirit and life. It is His to unfold to the heart the power and reality of the written word and to bring it to our remembrance in the opportune moment as the lamp of guidance or the sword of defense in the hour of temptation. He "will remind you of everything I have said to you" (John 14:26). This is the blessed ministry of the personal Holy Spirit, and those who walk with Him shall find the Bible an ever-new volume and the very light of life.

A prominent member of the House of Representatives, speaking about the inestimable value of the National Library of Congress, was asked how it was possible for a busy member, without much study and labor, to know how to use it effectively and to be able always to find the right volume or page where a given subject was discussed. "Oh," he replied, "that is made perfectly easy for us by

our invaluable librarian who knows every book
and subject. All we have to do is to send a little
page from our desk in the House with a note to
him requesting the best authority on any subject
we require, and he immediately comes back with
the right book and marked at the very spot where
we need the information."

Blessed be God, we have a divine Librarian who
understands the Bible better than we ever can and
who has come to be our Monitor and Guide, not
only into its meaning but also into its practical application to every need of life. "But when he, the
Spirit of truth, comes, he will guide you into all
truth" (John 16:13) and "will remind you of everything I [Christ] have said to you" (14:26).

The Light of Revelation

It is not enough to have a good light; we must
also have the organs of vision or it is of no use. And
we must have them in perfect condition. Now the
Holy Spirit comes to be to us sight as well as light.
As we walk in Him we shall be enabled to know
the will of God as revealed in the Scriptures by a
true spiritual apprehension and from the very
standpoint of God's own mind and thought.

In the chapter from which our text is taken Paul
uses a very fine analogy: "For who among men
knows the thoughts of a man except the man's
spirit within him? In the same way no one knows
the thoughts of God except the Spirit of God" (1
Corinthians 2:11). You might sit down and talk to
your dog about the latest book, and explain to him

in the clearest manner its wonderful teachings, but he would not understand a word—not from any defect in the truth but because he has not the mind of a man to understand the things of a man. Even so, you might sit down and talk to an intellectual about spiritual truth—even the most brilliant man one can imagine—and he would not comprehend it because such truth belongs to a higher sphere.

The only way by which that dog could understand you would be for you to impart to him a human mind, and the only way that man can understand the things of God is for God to impart to him the divine mind. Therefore, the apostle Paul says, "The man without the Spirit does not accept the things that come from the Spirit of God, for they are foolishness to him, and he cannot understand them, because they are spiritually discerned" (1 Corinthians 2:14). "But we have the mind of Christ" (2:16).

This is the special work of the Holy Spirit—to give to us a new spiritual vision and organ of apprehension so that the soul directly perceives divine things and realities. Perhaps the first effect of this divine illumination is that the things of God become intensely real and stand out with vividness and distinctness, like figures cut in relief on the wall. The person of Christ, the light of His countenance, the distinct sweetness of His Spirit, "the peace of God, which transcends all understanding" (Philippians 4:7), the joy of the Lord and the heavenly world all become to the heart more actual and intensely vivid than the things we see with our outward eyes and touch with our human hands. Because of this we can say of Christ, as did John, "That which . . . we have seen with our eyes, which we have looked at and our hands have touched—this we proclaim concerning the Word of life" (1 John 1:1). This is the true meaning of this whole chapter. It is not a description of heavenly glories which we are going to see by-and-by but of present revelations which the natural eye has not seen, the material ear hath not heard and the human heart hath not conceived, but "God has revealed it to us by his Spirit. The Spirit searches all things, even the deep things of God" (1 Corinthians 2:10).

In the first chapter of Ephesians, the apostle Paul has given us a sublime view of the effect of this inward illumination upon the heart.

> I have not stopped giving thanks for you, remembering you in my prayers. I keep asking that the God of our Lord Jesus Christ, the glorious Father, may give you the Spirit of wisdom and revelation, so that you may know him better. I pray also that the eyes of your heart may be enlightened in order that you may know the hope to which he has called you, the riches of his glorious inheritance in the saints, and his incomparably great power for us who believe. That power is like the working of his mighty strength, which he exerted in Christ when he raised

him from the dead and seated him at his
right hand in the heavenly realms, far above
all rule and authority, power and dominion,
and every title that can be given, not only in
the present age but also in the one to come.
(Ephesians 1:16-21)

"Which is his body, the fullness of him who fills
everything in every way" (1:23).

"And God raised us up with Christ and seated
us with him in the heavenly realms in Christ Jesus, in order that in the coming ages he might
show the incomparable riches of his grace, expressed in his kindness to us in Christ Jesus" (2:6-
7).

Here we find it is not the eyes of our intellect,
but the eyes of the heart that are to be illuminated,
and when so quickened by the Spirit of revelation
in the knowledge of Him, we shall understand
what is the hope of our calling and glorious privi-
leges and prospects which we are to inherit in
Christ.

The riches of the glory of His inheritance are
not only for us, but even in us now. We shall be
stirred with a realization of the exceeding greatness of His power toward us and for us. We shall
rise to an adequate conception of the mighty
things that we may dare to claim of Him; especially shall we see the full meaning of Christ's resurrection and ascension. We shall see Him lifted
up, not only above the grave and the burden of
our guilt and sin, but far above all beings, all

forces of natural law, all might and dominion, and every name that is named, up to the very throne of God where all things are under His feet. Not only so, but we shall see ourselves lifted up above our sins and fears and sorrows and enemies and difficulties and imperfections until we, too, are sitting with Him far above all principality, might and dominion, in the heavenly places in Christ Jesus—as safe and triumphant as if we were already in heaven and had been there for ten thousand years.

Such a view takes the sting out of life and stimulates to higher aspirations and victories, conflicts and service. But we must first perceive our inheritance before we can claim it, and as we look out upon all the fullness of His promise and provision we arise and walk through the land in all the length and breadth of it and make it our own. Under this divine light the promise of God grows strangely real, and the heart swells with faith and confidence. Doctrines which in the abstract we could not understand become simple and living realities. The profound truth of Trinity changes in the personal and sweet fellowship of the Father, the Son and the Holy Spirit. The doctrine of sanctification ceases to perplex and discourage, and becomes a simple experience of union with Jesus and abiding in Him. The mightiest supernatural works of Christ even in our bodies cease to be strange and incredible. The doctrine of His personal coming becomes a bright and personal expectation, and the whole world of spiritual things is more real to us in our own consciousness.

Sometimes the vision opens upon our own hearts and we are permitted to see their failures, imperfections and needs, but under the light of God this is never discouraging because there always comes with it the revelation of Him who is the supply of every need and the provision for every defect of sin. Satan's pictures of our sins are terrible and always depressing, but the light of heaven reveals our errors only to heal them, and brings such sweetness and rest that we can only thank Him for making greater room for His all-sufficiency.

Sometimes, too, the curtain is lifted upon the heavenly world, and some souls whom God can trust are permitted, like Paul, to be brought so near that they behold what it is unlawful for a man to utter and know not whether they are in the body or out of the body. Let no one covet such experiences, for they bring with them many a thorn in the flesh, lest we be exalted above measure. And above all let us not seek with morbid curiosity to intrude into things which do not belong to our simple sphere of humble duty. Rather let us seek the light that is practical and useful.

And yet, if God gives the higher visions at times—and even lifts the veil of things to come for humble and holy souls who dwell close to the gates of heaven—let us not wonder or question. Let us use such glimpses of glory as the mariner uses the burst of sunlight that sometimes pierces through the skies that have been clouded for weeks, and sails by the observations of that hour, through all the coming days of cloud and storm.

3) *The Light of Guidance*

The Holy Spirit is promised to us as our personal Guide in the path of life, "because those who are led by the Spirit of God are sons of God" (Romans 8:14). Some persons are so zealous for the Word of God that they deny any direct guidance of the Spirit apart from the Word. If we truly believe the Word itself we will be forced to accept its distinct statements that the personal presence of God is given to the humble and obedient disciple for the needed direction in every step of life. "I will instruct you and teach you in the way you should go; I will counsel you and watch over you" (Psalm 32:8). "The LORD will guide you always" (Isaiah 58:11). "When he has brought out all his own, he goes on ahead of them, and his sheep follow him because they know his voice" (John 10:4). "In all your ways acknowledge him, and he will make your paths straight" (Proverbs 3:6).

We find the apostle Paul constantly recognizing the personal direction of the Holy Spirit even in matters where there was no distinct direction in the Word. The whole course of Paul's missionary journeys was ordered by the personal direction of the Lord. Being sent forth, we are told, by the Holy Spirit, he and Barnabas sailed to Cyprus. A little later the same Spirit restrained them from preaching in Bithynia and Asia and led them from Troas to Philippi to begin their European ministry. Still later, we are told that he purposed in the Spirit to go to Jerusalem and Rome, and none of the perils of the way could afterward turn him aside from that which had come to him as the voice of God. No life was ever more practical, sensible and scriptural than Paul's, and yet none more constantly recognized the supernatural direction of the Holy Spirit. The methods of divine guidance are various.

The Spirit guides us by the Scriptures, by their general principles and teachings and by bringing to us special passages from the Word, either impressing them on our hearts through the law of mental suggestion or by various ways fitted to emphasize a passage as a divine message to our hearts.

He also guides us by His own direct voice when necessary. We must not, however, expect the special and remarkable intimations of the Holy Spirit at all times or when we have sufficient light from other sources. There is danger of fanaticism here. We have no right to ask God to give us a special revelation of His will where either the light of our own common sense or the teaching of Scripture have already made the matter sufficiently plain.

For example, it would be foolishness to expect the Lord to show us by a direct message whether we ought to get up in the morning, to take our proper food, to attend to our daily business, to keep the Sabbath or to perform the ordinary acts of kindness, courtesy and necessity—to pay our debts and to love our neighbor. All these things the Spirit has already told us and it would be an impertinence to expect Him to come with a new revelation every time.

In addition, we cannot expect the Holy Spirit to reveal to us directly whether God will forgive us our sins or sanctify our souls, because these things He has already explicitly promised us. We can expect no added witness of the Spirit until we have first believed and acted upon His Word. Then the Spirit will follow this by a confirming voice and an inward assurance of the fulfillment of His promise. Many persons expect the Spirit to come to them with the assurance of forgiveness and salvation before they have even believed the promises that He has already spoken.

We may also add this in regard to prayer for physical healing. When we are living in accordance with His Word, it does not require a special revelation of the will of God but simply a belief in the revelation already made in the Scriptures and in His promises of healing through faith in Christ.

But where the matter is one on which the Scriptures have not spoken distinctly, and the circumstances are so peculiar as to require direct and new light, He has distinctly promised that He will lead us in the right way wherein we shall not stumble. He has said, "If on some point you think differently, that too God will make clear to you" (Philippians 3:15).

The Holy Spirit guides us most frequently by intuitions of our sanctified judgment and the conclusions of our minds. To this end He leads us with the quiet assurance of acting in perfect freedom and naturalness and yet of being influenced by the presence and suggestion of His own Spirit. Under such circumstances the mind and judgment are perfectly simple and natural. The thoughts come as our own, with a delightful tranquility and certainty, and a sort of intuition that it is the right thing to do, and yet the secret consciousness that it is not our wisdom but has been somehow reflected upon the soul by another. It is not so much the Spirit speaking to us as the Spirit speaking with us as part of our very consciousness, so that it is not two minds, but one.

The truly consecrated spirit may expect to be thus held and influenced by the divine wisdom. It will often find itself restrained from things by an inward reluctance or repulsion which it cannot fully explain, and led to other things by a strong and distinct inclination and sense of rightness and fitness which later prove, by the result, to have been the directing presence of God. Of course, there must be real consecration and holy vigilance in such a walk, to guard against our own impressions and inclinations in cases where they are not the intimations of the Spirit's will.

We are sometimes taught that we are guided by providences. A devout mind will, of course, always have regard to the external providences of God and will be habitually watching to see His hand in everything that occurs. However, it would be very dangerous to allow ourselves to be directed by outward events apart from the distinct leadings of God in our spirit and by His Word. We shall find ourselves led to go as frequently in the face of circumstances as to follow the favoring gales of outward events.

Most of the important events and accomplished purposes in the lives of God's servants, as recorded in the Scriptures, were in direct opposition to all the circumstances that were occurring around them. Take, for example, the life of David. From the very first time that he received the call of God to recognize himself as Israel's future king, everything in his life for nearly 10 years seemed to conspire to forbid any such expectation.

Again, consider the life of Paul. We find him directly led by the Holy Spirit to cross the Hellespont and begin his ministry in Greece. Instead of being met by open doors, everything opposed until at last he found himself scourged and bound, a helpless prisoner in a Roman dungeon. Had he been watching for the guidance of circumstances, he would have concluded that he had made a mistake and would have hastened to get away. On the contrary, he believed more firmly that God had led him, and soon the very circumstances were conquered and transformed by the victorious power of faith. Again he was led to Jerusalem and Rome, but from that moment everything opposed him. All along the way the people of God even seemed to throw themselves across his path.

At Ephesus they wanted him to remain to preach the gospel in the very place where a year before he had tried in vain to enter. Instead of recognizing this as a providence that ought to change his purpose, he quietly deferred his work in Ephesus and pressed on to Jerusalem. Again and again on his way the very prophets of the Lord warned him against visiting Jerusalem and pleaded with him to abandon the dangerous purpose which perhaps would cost him his life. He only replied, "Why are you weeping and breaking my heart? I am ready not only to be bound, but also to die in Jerusalem for the name of the Lord Jesus" (Acts 21:13). When he arrived at Jerusalem all that had been intimated came to pass. Instead of being received by his countrymen, he was mobbed and nearly killed. Still he pressed on and the Lord met him at night in his dungeon to assure him of His protection and direction.

Next he was detained at Caesarea for two whole years, languishing in a prison. But instead of doubting his divine direction he looked steadily ahead and used the delay as an occasion of service for the Master.

At length he embarked for Rome. Even then the storm pursued him and the wild Euroclydon threatened to engulf him in the depths of the sea. Still he faltered not in his purpose but rose majestically above the storm and carried even the lives of his fellow passengers, on the wings of his mighty faith, above disaster and destruction. After Paul narrowly escaped shipwreck on the shores of Malta, a viper from the ashes of a fire fastened itself upon his hand—it seemed as though earth and hell had determined to prevent his reaching Rome—but he only flung it off and suffered no harm. And at length he marched up the Appian Way, more like a conqueror than a prisoner, thanking God and taking courage as he realized that not one word of all God's promise and direction had failed.

This is the manner in which we should always interpret the providences of God: Instead of yielding to opposition or following that which seems to favor us, let us press firmly on in the path of conviction and obedience, and our way shall be established and our very difficulties become the occasions of our greatest triumphs.

Let us notice also some of the principles and conditions of divine guidance.

The first is a *surrendered spirit*. Before we can know His will we must always first yield our own. "He guides the humble in what is right and teaches them his way" (Psalm 25:9).

Next, there must be a *readiness to obey*. He will not give us light unless we mean to follow it; to do so would only add to our condemnation: "If anyone chooses to do God's will, he will find out" (John 7:17). "Let us acknowledge the LORD; let us press on to acknowledge him" (Hosea 6:3).

In addition, we must *trust His guidance*. We must believe that He is with us and directing us. We must lean upon His arm with all our heart and implicitly look up into His face and expect Him to be true to us. We must also be of those "who by constant use have trained themselves to distinguish good from evil" (Hebrews 5:14). Sometimes our mistakes will become most instructive to us by showing us the places where we have erred and by saving us from repeating the mistake afterward with more serious consequences.

We must learn to distinguish between mere impressions and the deeper convictions of the entire judgment under the light of the Spirit, and between the voice of the Shepherd and that of the spirit of error. This He will teach us, and teach us more and more perfectly through experience.

We shall have to learn also to walk with Him when we cannot understand the way. His path is often a way that we have not known, and the answer to our prayer may seem to lead us directly contrary to our expectation and to the ultimate issue.

At one time I was led to ask the Lord for a special building as a residence, and received full assurance that it would be given. Almost immediately it was sold to a person who insisted on occupying it himself and refused under any circumstances to part with it. After much prayer I was led to consent, most unwillingly, and to accept instead of the house I had really wanted another owned by this very man. It was so distasteful to me that on the night I was to sign the lease I walked repeatedly past the door before I could bring myself to enter.

Finally, in simple obedience to the Holy Spirit, I did. To my surprise, the man met me and said that on that very afternoon he had been led to change his mind. While attending the funeral of an old friend, a strange dread had come over him about occupying the house he had purchased and he had just decided to let me have it on terms more favorable than I could have expected had not God interposed. Thus, as I went forward in the path of simple obedience, by a way that I could not understand, the true way opened up, and it was sheer blessing and delight. The most remarkable feature of it was that the house God provided later became the place where all the work of the Lord began. God signally chose the place for His work and put His seal upon it as a pattern of the providences which we should afterward expect.

So still, "through fears, through clouds, through storms, He gently clears our way."

Let us trust His guiding hand, and "follow the Lamb wherever he goes" (Revelation 14:4).

Light for Service

"[F]or it will not be you speaking, but the Spirit of your Father speaking through you" (Matthew 10:20). "For I will give you words and wisdom that none of your adversaries will be able to resist or contradict" (Luke 21:15). "If anyone speaks, he should do it as one speaking the very words of God. If anyone serves, he should do it with the strength God provides, so that in all things God may be praised through Jesus Christ" (1 Peter 4:11). "Do not say, 'I am only a child.' You must go to everyone I send you to and say whatever I command you" (Jeremiah 1:7).

"Then the LORD reached out his hand and touched my mouth and said to me, 'Now, I have put my words in your mouth'" (Jeremiah 1:9). "The Sovereign LORD has given me an instructed tongue, to know the word that sustains the weary. He wakens me morning by morning, wakens my ear to listen like one being taught" (Isaiah 50:4). This was the secret of even Christ's ministry. "These words you hear are not my own; they belong to the Father who sent me" (John 14:24). "I judge only as I hear" (5:30).

Before we can speak God's messages we must learn to listen. The opened ear comes before the opened mouth. It is very hard sometimes to die to our own thoughts and elaborate preparations for service and to be free and open for God to use us as vessels meet for the Master's use. Sometimes He has to humble us by showing us the barrenness of all our best intellectual work, and then lead us to receive the living messages of His Holy Spirit. Sometimes we may think the message very unworthy and almost unsuitable, but God loves to take "the things that are not—to nullify the things that are, so that no one may boast before him" (1 Corinthians 1:28-29).

A woman, greatly used of God, relates how she was once distinctly sent by the Lord to take a certain train. When she arrived at the station the train was crowded and the guard told her she could not get on. Still she waited, having learned that a point-blank refusal is often the best evidence of God's working. Suddenly, just as the train was about to leave, the guard came to her and hurried her into a car which had just been put on. There she found herself sitting beside a young man. Immediately the thought came, "This is the service the Lord has sent me to do." After they had talked for a time she introduced the subject of personal religion. His response was a haughty, "My family objects to my being talked to on such subjects."

"My friend," she replied, "I would have thought that this was not a question for your family, but for you."

"Then," he answered even more stiffly, "I object to being talked to on such questions." It seemed as though the way of service was blocked, and yet the unerring Spirit had led her there.

The thought came to her that she should give him a tract. As she searched through her pockets she found that she had forgotten to bring them.

Suddenly, disturbed by her movement, her small train case fell to the floor and all its contents were poured in disorder at their feet. The young man came to her aid and as they picked up and replaced the articles she noticed a single tract that had fallen out with the other things. Even as she picked it up she felt that it would never do, for it concerned a young man who had been saved from shipwreck. The same unerring Guide whispered to her to put it in his hands and ask him to read it.

The young man took the tract, having become more relaxed as they talked, and as he read the title his face became deathly pale. Before he had read the second page he was in tears. Turning to her he cried, "Who told you about me?"

"Why, no one," she answered. "What do you mean?"

"Someone must have told you," he said. "Didn't you know that only last week I was rescued from shipwreck?"

It was the arrow of God, and His trusting and obedient servant had not been allowed to err. The message reached the heart and the young man received Christ.

This is the true secret of effectual service. When He becomes to us the Wonderful Counselor, we shall always find Him also the Mighty God.

The Spirit of Holiness

[W]ho have been chosen according to the fore-knowledge of God the Father, through the sanctifying work of the Spirit, for obedience to Jesus Christ. (1 Peter 1:2)

It would throw a flood of light on the perplexing doctrine of election if we would remember when thinking of this subject that we are elected by God, not unto salvation unconditionally and absolutely, but unto holiness. We are predestinated to be conformed to the image of His Son. It is idle and unscriptural, therefore, to talk about being elected to salvation irrespective of our faith and obedience. We are elected to obedience and sprinkling of the blood of Christ and are summoned, therefore, to make our calling and election sure by pressing on into the fullness of the grace of Christ. This work of sanctification is especially

the work of the Holy Spirit. Let us look carefully
at the principles that lie at the foundation of it,
and its connection with the person and work of
the Holy Spirit.

The holiness to which we are called and into
which we are introduced by the Holy Spirit is not
the restoration of Adamic perfection or the recovery of the nature we lost by the Fall. It is a higher
holiness, even the very nature of God Himself,
and the indwelling of Jesus Christ, the second
Adam, to whose perfect likeness we shall be restored through the work of redemption. We are
predestined to be conformed to the image of His
Son. This will determine all our subsequent conclusions in the consideration of this subject. Sanctification is not the perfection of human character,
but the impartation of the divine nature and the
union of the human soul with the person of
Christ, the new Head of redeemed humanity.

Our sanctification has been purchased for us
through the redemption of Christ. "Because by
one sacrifice he has made perfect forever those
who are being made holy" (Hebrews 10:14).
When He came He said, "Here I am, I have
come—it is written about me in the scroll. I desire
to do your will, O my God; your law is within my
heart" (Psalm 40:7-8). "And by that will, we have
been made holy through the sacrifice of the body
of Jesus Christ once for all" (Hebrews 10:10).

Our sanctification, therefore, as well as our jus-
tification, was included in the finished work of
Christ, and it is a free gift of His grace to every

ransomed soul that accepts it in accordance with His Word and will. It is one of our redemption rights in Christ, and we may claim it by faith as freely as our forgiveness. For He "who gave himself for us to redeem us from all wickedness and to purify for himself a people that are his very own, eager to do what is good" (Titus 2:14).

It is the office of the Holy Spirit to lead us into the full redemption of Jesus Christ and therefore into holiness. In bringing this about, the Holy Spirit leads us first to see our need of sanctification. This He does by a twofold revelation. First, He shows us the divine will for our sanctification and the necessity for our becoming holy if we would please God. By nature and tradition, many persons are prone to take a very different view of this subject. They regard the experience of holiness as a sort of exceptional life for a few distinguished Christians and not expected of all the disciples of Christ.

But the awakened and startled mind discovers, in the light of Scripture and of the Holy Spirit, the falseness of this delusion and the inflexible terms in which God's Word requires that all His people should be holy in heart and life. In the searching light of truth it trembles as it reads, "[W]ithout holiness no one will see the Lord" (Hebrews 12:14). "Nothing impure will ever enter it, nor will anyone who does what is shameful or deceitful" (Revelation 21:27). "Blessed are those who wash their robes, that they may have the right to the tree of life and may go through the gates into the city" (Revelation 22:14). "He who walks righteously and speaks what is right. . . . Your eyes will see the king in his beauty and view a land that stretches afar" (Isaiah 33:15, 17). "Who may ascend the hill of the LORD? Who may stand in his holy place? He who has clean hands and a pure heart" (Psalm 24:3-4). "Be holy, because I am holy" (1 Peter 1:16). "Be perfect, therefore, as your heavenly Father is perfect" (Matthew 5:48). "I write this to you so that you will not sin" (1 John 2:1). "No one who lives in him keeps on sinning. No one who continues to sin has either seen him or known him" (3:6).

At this point the soul is compelled to face a very solemn crisis. Either it must accept the Word of God literally and implicitly or it must turn it aside by human tradition and explain away its plainest and most emphatic teachings. In so doing we render it of no effect in any of its promises or commands and enter upon a course which must end in practical infidelity.

The latter alternative is taken by many; they content themselves with saying such a standard is impossible. Nobody has ever reached it, and God does not actually mean it or require it. The result is that the Word of God becomes uncertain to them in all its messages, and a practical faith ceases to be possible. But the other alternative drives the soul, if honestly faced, to self-despair; it can find no such holiness in itself, and no power to produce it.

The first effect, it is true, generally is to stir up

the awakened heart to attempt a better life and try to work out a holiness such as God requires, by resolutions, outward amendments, perhaps many inward exercises, self-examinations and purposes of righteousness and holiness.

After a time, however, there is a sense of failure and disappointment. Perhaps the man becomes a Pharisee and deludes himself into the idea that he is complying with the divine standard. If the Holy Spirit is doing His office work thoroughly, he will soon become disgusted with his own righteousness and his utter inability even to reach his own standard. Some crucial test will come which he cannot meet, some command which strikes at the roots of his natural inclinations and requires the sacrifice of his dearest idols. Then the heart will break down, and the will shrink or rebel.

This was the experience of the apostle Paul. For the time he thought he had attained unto the righteousness of the law, "but when the commandment came, sin sprang to life and I died" (Romans 7:9). The Lord said, "You shall not covet" (Exodus 20:17), and instantly his throbbing heart awoke with all the intensity of its natural life to a thousand evil desires, all the stronger because they were forbidden, until in despair he cried out, "We know that the law is spiritual; but I am unspiritual" (Romans 7:14). "What a wretched man I am! Who will rescue me from this body of death?" (Romans 7:24). This is the very preparation for sanctification. He is just on the verge of deliverance. He has finally found his helplessness. He

has come to the bottom of the ladder of self-renunciation. It is to such a soul that the Master is
saying, "Blessed are the poor in spirit, for theirs is
the kingdom of heaven" (Matthew 5:3). "Blessed
are those who hunger and thirst for righteousness,
for they will be filled" (5:6).

God came to Job in the revelation of his own
worthlessness until he cried, "I despise myself"
(Job 42:6). He came to Isaiah, and the prophet's
response was, "Woe to me! . . . For I am a man of
unclean lips" (Isaiah 6:5). Happy the man who can
see himself at his worst without, on the one hand,
attempting to excuse his failure, or on the other,
giving up in despair. For such a one the Holy
Spirit waits to bring the next stage of His work of
sanctification, namely, the revelation of Jesus
Christ Himself as our sanctification.

It is the purpose of God that the Person of Jesus
shall be to us the embodiment of all that there is in
God and salvation.

Sanctification is not a mere human experience
or state but is the reception of the Person of Christ
as the very substance of our spiritual life. For He
"who has become for us wisdom from God—that
is, our righteousness, holiness and redemption" (1
Corinthians 1:30). It is not a wealthy friend ad-
vancing us the money to pay our debts. It is the
Friend coming into our business and assuming it
Himself, with all its burdens and liabilities, while
we simply become subordinate and receive all our
needs from Him. This was the glad cry which
Paul sent back the moment he had reached the

depths of self-despair: "Thanks be to God—through Jesus Christ our Lord" (Romans 7:25). It is the Holy Spirit's function to reveal Him. "[T]he Spirit will take from what is mine and make it known to you" (John 16:15).

And now in the light of His revealing we behold Christ, the perfect One, who walked in sinless perfection through the world in His incarnation, waiting to come and enter our hearts and dwell in us, and walk in us as the very substance of our new life, while we simply abide in Him and walk in His very steps. It is not merely imitating an example, but it is living the very life of another. It is to have the very Person of Christ possessing our being—the thoughts of Christ, the desires of Christ, the will of Christ, the faith of Christ, the purity of Christ, the love of Christ, the unselfishness of Christ, the single aim of Christ, the obedience of Christ, the humility of Christ, the submission of Christ, the meekness of Christ, the patience of Christ, the gentleness of Christ, the zeal of Christ—and the works of Christ manifest in our mortal flesh.

Then we shall be able to say, "I live; yet not I, but Christ liveth in me" (Galatians 2:20, KJV). When the Holy Spirit thus reveals Him to the heart we can say, as a saint once said after such a vision, "I have had such a sight of Christ that I never can be discouraged again."

The Spirit not only reveals Christ, but He actually brings Him to occupy and abide in the heart. It is not enough to see; we must receive Him and e personally united to Him through the Spirit. In order to do this there must be, on our part, a complete surrender and self-renunciation followed by a definite act of appropriating faith. By it we receive the Lord Jesus Christ and become filled with the Holy Spirit. In both of these we are led and enabled by the Holy Spirit. Through His gracious influence we present our bodies a living sacrifice, yield ourselves unto God in unreserved consecration, hand over to Him the old life of self and sin to be slain and buried forever and offer ourselves to His absolute ownership, possession and disposition, unconditionally and irrevocably. The more definite and thorough this act of surrender, the more complete and permanent will be the result. It is true that at best it will be an imperfect consecration and will need His merit to make it acceptable. But He will accept a sincere and single desire and will add His own perfect consecration to our imperfect act, making it acceptable to the Father through His grace.

It is most blessed to know that in the very first act of a consecrated life we are not alone, but He Himself becomes our consecration, as He will afterward become our obedience and our strength, step by step, to the end.

Having surrendered ourselves to Him for His sanctifying grace, we must now accept Him in His fullness and believe that He becomes to us all that we take Him for. We must acknowledge that we are now owned, accepted, possessed, cleansed

and sanctified by His indwelling, and that He is
saying to us—and recording our glad amen, without reserve, to every word of it—"You are already
clean because of the word I have spoken to you"
(John 15:3). "The blood of Jesus, his Son, purifies
us from all sin" (1 John 1:7).

The Holy Spirit next seals this act of union by
His own manifested presence and the baptism of
His love and power. Before we can expect to receive this, however, we must simply believe the
promise of Christ, resting in the certainty of our
acceptance and consecration, and begin to act by
implicit faith in Him as already in our hearts.
When we do, the Holy Spirit will not withhold
the conscious witness of our blessing a moment
longer than is really necessary for the testing and
establishing of our faith.

He will become to us a most blessed and personal reality, and it shall be true of us, as the Master Himself promised, after the Comforter has
come, that "[o]n that day you will realize that I am
in my Father, and you are in me, and I am in
you." (John 14:20). The soul will be filled with the
delightful consciousness of the presence of God,
sometimes as a spirit of ineffable rest and holy serenity, sometimes as a spirit of unutterable holiness, filling the heart as with the searching and
consuming fire of divine purity. Sometimes the
consciousness will be that of an intense hatred of
sin and a spirit of self-renunciation and holy vigilance. Sometimes it will be a spirit of love, an intense consciousness of the divine approval and of

God's delight in us and love to us, until the heart is melted with the sense of His tenderness. Sometimes it is a spirit of unspeakable joy and rapture, continuing for days, until the very tides of God's love seem to swell within the heart with unutterable glory. Sometimes it is a very quiet, simple consciousness, prompting one to abide in Christ in great simplicity for every instant's need; there is no transcendent emotion, but simply a satisfying awareness of Christ sufficient for our practical life.

In every case it is really satisfaction, and we know that the Lord has come to abide with us forever, and be our all-sufficiency and our everlasting portion.

The Holy Spirit now begins to lead us in the steps of a holy life. We find it is to be maintained by the moment. We have no crystalized and stereotyped condition of self-centered life, but we have Christ for the present moment and must constantly abide in Him. We must walk in the Spirit, and we shall not fulfill the lusts of the flesh. We must be filled with the Spirit, and we shall have no room for sin.

It is now that we find the importance of walking in the Spirit and maintaining steadfastly the habit of obedience and fellowship with Him as the essential condition of the life of holiness. One of the first and most important lessons is to heed His voice. Obedience to the Spirit is life and peace, but obedience to the flesh is death. The Spirit is given, we are told, to them that obey Him. The disobedient and inattentive heart will find His fellowship constantly liable to be interrupted and suspended. The life of holiness is not a mere abstract state, but a mosaic made up of a thousand minute details of life and action.

A Christian lady, while thinking of the subject of sanctification, found herself suddenly absorbed in a sort of waking vision in which she seemed to see a builder erecting an edifice of stone. First, she saw a deep excavation and at the bottom a solid rock on which the house was to be placed. Across this rock was written the name of Christ, with the words, "For no one can lay any foundation other than the one already laid, which is Jesus Christ" (1 Corinthians 3:11).

Then a derrick swung before her eyes and a stone was deposited in the rear of the building. It was a very plain-looking block of granite, with no decoration whatever on its face. As it was deposited in an obscure portion of the wall there appeared the word "Humility." Next the derrick swung around to the front of the wall and planted another foundation stone on the principal corner, and the name of this was "Faith."

The walls now rose rapidly; block after block of enduring granite was laid and cemented and finally fashioned into a magnificent arch surmounted by a beautiful keystone, the loveliest stone in all the building. Across it was written the name "Love." Between these principal stones the interstices were filled with innumerable small pieces of every size and shape. These bore the names of qualities of the Christian character, such as meekness, gentleness, temperance, forbearance, patience, considerateness, serenity, courtesy, cheerfulness. The whole facade was spanned by one glowing word in golden letters, "Sanctification."

The prejudices of a lifetime were at once removed and she saw the loveliness of a holy life and character and the true meaning of the word that she had so long misconceived and disliked.

This, then, is the Holy Spirit's work in the life of holiness. It is much more than a mere blank sheet of spotless white: It is the living portrait wrought out upon that sheet in all the features of holy loveliness and all the positive qualities of a practical and beautiful Christian life. "But the fruit of the Spirit is love, joy, peace, patience, kindness, goodness, faithfulness, gentleness and self-control" (Galatians 5:22-23). "[W]hatever is true, whatever is noble, whatever is right, whatever is pure, whatever is lovely, whatever is admirable—if anything is excellent or praiseworthy—think about such things" (Philippians 4:8).

These things the Holy Spirit comes to transcribe in our hearts and to reflect in our lives. Yet these qualities are not our own in any sense in which we could claim them as the result of our own goodness, or rest in them as permanent, personal attributes. They are rather to be regarded as the grace of Christ, supplied to us from His own indwelling Spirit moment by moment. "From the fullness of his grace we have all received one blessing after another" (John 1:16). This is the grace to produce in us all the varied adornments of the Christian life.

As Peter expresses it, "that you may declare the praises of him who called you out of darkness into his wonderful light" (1 Peter 2:9). These are the bridal robes which are granted to the Lamb's wife, "Fine linen, bright and clean, was given her to wear" (Revelation 19:8). These are like Rebecca's ornaments and veil, which are not woven by her hands but brought her by Eliezer from Isaac himself, and which she had simply to put on and wear.

In the same way the Holy Spirit, typified by Abraham's servant, brings to us the wedding robe and supplies to us day by day the special garment that fits us for each new situation and emergency. We simply put on the Lord Jesus and walk in Him as our all-sufficiency for every place of duty and trial.

The Spirit is ever present to reveal Him to us in every new aspect of grace and fullness. Every new need or failure is an invitation to take Him in greater fullness and prove in a higher sense that He is indeed able to save to the uttermost and keep to the end.

Not only does the Holy Spirit lead us into the positive graces of the Christian life, but He also keeps us perpetually cleansed from all the stains of spiritual defilement and even from the effects of temptation and evil suggestion. If sin should touch the heart even for a moment, He is there to reveal instantly the evil and in the same flash of light to present and apply a remedy. "But if we walk in the light, as he is in the light, . . . the blood of Jesus, his Son, purifies us from all sin" (1 John 1:7).

Thus the soul, like the pebble in the stream, allows the perpetual cleansing of His life. Indeed, we may walk so close to Him that before the sin is even admitted, before the temptation has reached the citadel of the will and becomes our own act, it is repelled at the entrance and does not become our sin. He has promised to keep us as the apple of His eye.

Even as the eyelash is so constructed that the very approach of the smallest particle of dust causes the eye instantly to close and repel the intruding substance, so the gentle Holy Spirit instinctively guards the heart and conscience from willful sin. There is something, however, even in the presence of temptation and the surrounding atmosphere of a sin-defiled world that spreads contagion around us. It is necessary that even this should be constantly cleansed, even as the falling showers wash away the dust from the pavements and trees and purify the summer air. The Holy Spirit constantly does this, and diffuses through the sanctified heart the freshness and sweetness of the heavenly atmosphere.

We find in the Old Testament types a beautiful provision for the cleansing of the people, even from the touch of the dead, through the water of separation (Numbers 19). This meaningful ordinance was a type of the Holy Spirit applying to us the atonement of Christ—cleansing us habitually from the very breath and even the indirect contagion of surrounding evil. Should our old, dead carnal nature touch us, or the atmosphere of sin surround us, we have constantly this water of separation. The moment we are sprinkled with it every effect is removed, as the rain revives the famished earth and causes the desert to blossom.

We must ever bear in mind, in tracing the Holy Spirit's work in the believer's heart, the distinction between purity of heart and maturity of character. From the moment that the soul is yielded to Christ in full surrender and He is received as its divine and indwelling life, we have His purity. The old, sinful self is reckoned dead and no longer recognized as our true self. There is a complete and eternal divorce; the old heart is now treated as if it no longer existed. Christ is recognized now as the true I—a life that is essentially pure and divine.

Although wholly separated from the old sinful life, the new spirit is still in its infancy and before it lie boundless stages of progress and development. The acorn is as complete in its parts as the oak of a thousand years, but not as fully developed. The soul, also, which has just received Christ as its abiding life and sanctification, is as wholly sanctified and as completely one with Him as Enoch or John is today, but not as mature. This is what we mean by Christian growth. We do not grow into holiness; we receive holiness in Christ as a complete, divine life—complete in all its parts from the beginning, and divine, as Christ is. But it is like the infant Christ in Mary's arms, and it has to grow up into all the fullness of the stature of perfect manhood in Christ.

This is the work of the Holy Spirit as the mother, nurse, teacher, educator and cherisher of our spiritual life. It is in this connection that we must learn to walk in the Spirit and rise with Him into "all the good pleasure of his goodness, and the work of faith with power" (2 Thessalonians 1:11, KJV), until we shall have reached the fullness of His own prayer for us:

> May the God of peace, who through the blood of the eternal covenant brought back from the dead our Lord Jesus, that great Shepherd of the sheep, equip you with everything good for doing his will, and may he work in us what is pleasing to him, through Jesus Christ, to whom be glory for ever and ever. Amen. (Hebrews 13:20-21)

The Spirit of Life

And if the Spirit of him who raised Jesus from the dead is living in you, he who raised Christ from the dead will also give life to your mortal bodies through his Spirit, who lives in you. (Romans 8:11)

What is life? The unsolved question of science and philosophy. What is it that makes the difference between the soaring bird, mounting the air on buoyant wing, and that little limp, broken thing that the hunter gathers up in his hands a moment later? What is the cause of this strange, terrible change? The galvanic battery can mimic some of the movements of life in muscle and limb, but when the current ceases the movement stops. In a few hours the flesh has yielded to the power of corruption and is dissolving into earth again.

What life does, we know; what it is baffles the scientists.

Science is approaching slowly the true center which the Bible gave us long ago. It is steadily reducing all vital force to one essential principle, perhaps electricity. The Bible has settled the question in regard to Him who is the source of life, "He is the true God and eternal life" (1 John 5:20). God is the fountain of life, and Christ is the life of God for men. Christ's life is the true source of life for the souls and bodies of His children. This life He imparts to us through the Holy Spirit who becomes, to the soul that is united to Him, the medium and the channel of vital union and communion with Christ, our Living Head. The Holy Spirit becomes to us the Spirit of life in Christ Jesus because He imparts to us the life of Jesus.

That He should be able to quicken our mortal bodies should not seem strange. As we have already intimated, even physical science has been learning, in some measure, to recognize life not so much as a matter of external organism and coarse material elements as of vital force.

Time has changed radically the methods of treatment known to medical science. Physicians now rely much more upon natural forces and resources and more subtle and vital elements to counteract the power of disease than formerly.

The influence of air and occupation, or surrounding circumstances and mental conditions— all these are given serious consideration. Today, health is recognized as the result of both inward forces and outward agencies. These are distinct approximations toward the higher truth, that the source of our strength must be looked for in the direct power and contact of that spiritual personality in whom "we live and move and have our being" (Acts 17:28).

This is the plain teaching of the Scriptures from beginning to end, and we shall probably be surprised to find how much is taught in its sacred pages regarding the relation of the Holy Spirit to our physical life.

The Part of the Holy Spirit in Creation

We know that the divine Spirit is recognized in the Scriptures as the direct agent in the original creation and the Spirit of life and order in the whole domain of nature and providence.

How strikingly this is described in the majestic psalm of nature, Psalm 104: "When you hide your face, they are terrified; when you take away their breath, they die and return to the dust. When you send your Spirit, they are created, and you renew the face of the earth" (104:29-30).

This is the power that formed the heavens with their bodies of light, that covers the woods and fields with robes of many-tinted glory, that animates the teeming world of insect and animal life, that breathed into man the breath of life at the beginning and still sustains his physical existence, and that has created all his mortal powers and endowments. Why should it be thought strange that He who made us should sustain us, restore us and "will also give life to your mortal bodies through his Spirit, who lives in you" (Romans 8:11).

The Work of the Holy Spirit in the Body in the Old Testament

We have a very remarkable pattern of physical life in one of the Old Testament biographies. It is the story of Samson, and it was directly intended as a lesson of the true nature and source of physical strength. Samson's stupendous power was not due to physical organization at all, but only and directly to the power and presence of the Holy Spirit. Note that in the very beginning of his strength it is repeatedly stated, "[A]nd the Spirit of the LORD began to stir him. . . . The Spirit of the LORD came upon him" (Judges 13:25; 14:6, 19).

When he was deserted by the Holy Spirit he was helpless in the hands of his enemies, but when he was filled with the superhuman power of God's Spirit he could carry away the gates of the city or hurl the walls of Dagon's temple upon the assembled thousands of his enemies.

The lesson of Samson's life is unmistakably a foreshadowing of the great New Testament truth that our bodily life as well as our spiritual has its root and nourishment in God. It teaches that, as we walk in separation from evil and in fellowship with Him, He "who raised Christ from the dead will also give life to your mortal bodies through his Spirit, who lives in you" (Romans 8:11).

3 The Part of the Holy Spirit in the Personal Ministry of Christ

It was He that performed the supernatural works of the Lord Jesus on earth. Not one miracle did He do until He received the baptism of the Holy Spirit. Then He said, "The Spirit of the Lord is on me, because . . . he hath sent me to heal the brokenhearted, . . . to set at liberty them that are bruised" (Luke 4:18 KJV). When His enemies attributed His miracles to the power of Satan, He distinctly declared that they were performed by the power of the Holy Spirit and added, "But if I drive out demons by the Spirit of God, then the kingdom of God has come upon you" (Matthew 12:28). And then He proceeded to charge them with the fatal sin against the Holy Spirit in attributing His works to Satan (12:31).

If, then, Christ cast out demons and wrought miracles by the power of the Holy Spirit, and it is the same Spirit who still abides in the church and dwells in the hearts and bodies of believers, why should it be thought strange that this same Almighty Spirit should work in our bodies the same works, and quicken them, as our text declares?

4 The Part of the Holy Spirit in the Apostolic Ministry and in the Permanent Enduement of the Church

It was not until the Holy Spirit descended

that the apostles were permitted to exercise their ministry in power, and all the mighty works that followed are distinctly attributed by Peter and the other apostles to His personal working. He quotes from the prophet Joel the distinct promise, "I will pour out my Spirit in those days" (Acts 2:18), and it is followed by the announcement of what shall ensue, "I will show wonders in the heaven above and signs on the earth below" (2:19).

It was after the Holy Spirit descended again, causing the meeting place to be shaken, that we read, "The apostles performed many miraculous signs and wonders among the people" (5:12). And it was through His continuing and supernatural presence that the divine gifts were to be manifested in the church to the end of the present dispensation. "There are different kinds of gifts, but the same Spirit" (1 Corinthians 12:4).

> To one there is given through the Spirit the message of wisdom, to another the message of knowledge by means of the same Spirit, to another faith by the same Spirit, to another gifts of healing by that one Spirit, to another miraculous powers. (12:8-10)

"All these are the work of one and the same Spirit, and he gives them to each one, just as he determines" (12:11).

It is evident that all the supernatural effects of Christianity are accomplished through the Holy

Spirit. It is His function to perpetuate in the church the very works that Christ performed through Him on earth, the Church being simply the body of the ascended Savior and the channel through which He is to work in the same divine manner. Jesus said, when He spoke of the coming of His Spirit: "I tell you the truth, anyone who has faith in me will do what I have been doing. He will do even greater things than these, because I am going to the Father" (John 14:12).

Why, then, should it seem strange that this blessed Spirit should do the very work He came to do, and still quicken our mortal bodies as He dwells within us?

The Special Ministry of the Holy Spirit for Our Bodies

In the sixth chapter of First Corinthians, the dignity and sacredness of the human body are very clearly presented as an argument against impurity in our social relations. "Do you not know," He asks, "that your bodies are members of Christ himself?" and then, "Do you not know that your body is a temple of the Holy Spirit?" (1 Corinthians 6:15, 19).

Earlier in this epistle He had spoken of the Spirit's ministry within us in a more spiritual sense (3:16-17) but here He refers explicitly to His union with our physical life and with the body of Jesus Christ as God's substitute. The body is for the Lord and the Lord for the body. It is the ministry of the Holy Spirit to unite our body to our

I's and to inhabit it and hold it in sacredness and purity for Him.

Let us distinctly understand that it is of our physical life that these Scriptures speak, not our spiritual. That is also united to Christ, but surely with so much teaching regarding that part of our being, we can afford to claim these specific references for that which was intended by them—our consecrated physical life.

The only way in which the simple and conclusive effect of our text can be turned aside is by attempting to apply it to the future resurrection, as sometimes has been done. It is therefore good that we look carefully at its connection and establish its true application on sound exegetical grounds.

The general connection of chapter 6 makes this very plain. No less an authority than John Calvin has proved that this passage cannot refer to the future resurrection, because the apostle is speaking, in this place, of the present work of the Holy Spirit in the believer, and it is not until much later that he advances to the future hopes that await us at the Lord's coming. The subject of the chapter is the blessed indwelling of the Holy Spirit in those who have yielded themselves wholly to Christ.

The first effect of His indwelling is given in the second verse: It is *deliverance from indwelling sin through the indwelling of the Holy Spirit.*

The second is *the new habit of obedience to the Spirit*, expressed so beautifully in Romans 8 by the expression, "[T]he mind controlled by the Spirit is life and peace" (Romans 8:6). "[T]hose who live in accordance with the Spirit have their minds set on what the Spirit desires" (8:5).

The third effect of the Spirit's indwelling is *His quickening life for our bodies,* and this is here described in the text.

In the previous verse the body as well as the soul is recognized as yielded up to death, and so reckoned as good as dead, that we no more depend upon its natural strength as sufficient. In contrast with this the Holy Spirit becomes its new life and quickens our mortal body by the same power which raised Christ from the dead. This follows later in the chapter in verses 14 and 15.

The blessed leading of the Holy Spirit through the experience of Christian life culminates at last in the realization of our future hope when we shall enter into the full redemption of the body at Christ's second coming (8:23). But concerning this full redemption of the body, we are told in this same verse that we have even now the first fruits of the Spirit. This is, of course, the quickening influence which the Spirit exercises in our mortal bodies even in this present life, and which is the foretaste of the full resurrection.

Thus, the very order of the chapter prepares us to apply the text to a present experience. John Calvin, as we have already stated, does so, but instead of recognizing that present Spirit as divine healing, of which probably the good reformer never thought, he regards it as the consecrating of our bodies to the service and glory of God—a sense, of course, which the word quicken does not bear.

This leads us to consider the meaning of the word "quicken." It would require a very strong inversion—or perversion—of the word to apply this term to the consecration of the body, for it literally means the reviving, stimulating, animating, invigorating of its strength.

The nearest parallel passage where it is employed is in this same epistle (Romans 4:17) where it is applied to the act which God performed in quickening the body of Abraham when he was past age, and also the vital organs of Sarah, his wife, so that Isaac was born contrary to nature.

In this case, neither Abraham nor Sarah were dead. Their vital systems were exhausted, and they were simply quickened, revived and renewed.

The word does not suggest the literal resurrection of the dead, but rather the reviving and restoring of strength when it is exhausted—precisely what is done when our failing health is renewed and our infirmities are healed by the indwelling power of the Holy Spirit through the name of Jesus.

It will make this conclusion still more obvious if we remember that it is our mortal bodies that are here described: not our souls at all, but our physical beings.

This, therefore, is a direct operation of the Holy Spirit upon our vital functions, organs and health. Any other application is contrary to the simple and natural meaning of the passage.

That this is not the resurrection body is certain from the fact that it is called the mortal body. A mortal body means a dying body, certainly not dead body, and still more certainly not a resurrected body. The bodies of the saints, when raised from the dead at Christ's coming, shall not be mortal bodies, but immortal, nor *can they die any more*, our Lord Himself has said.

The whole induction of proof is crowned by the clause *that dwelleth in us*. Now that must mean the present dwelling of the Holy Spirit in our present mortal bodies. It cannot mean our buried dust, for then the Spirit will not be dwelling in us. It is a process which is now going on through the indwelling and inworking of the Holy Spirit.

We might add to these thoughts the impressive one suggested by the terms, "the Spirit of him who raised Jesus from the dead" (Romans 8:11). This is the Spirit of a physical resurrection. The resurrection of Christ from the dead was a physical resurrection. His soul was not dead; it was His body that was raised from the tomb, and if it be the pattern of the Spirit's working in us, it must have reference to our body also.

We have not sufficiently realized the physical meaning of Christ's resurrection or given enough emphasis to the stupendous fact that He who came forth from that grave has become the physical head of our life, and that "we are members of his body" (Ephesians 5:30), and have a right to draw from His glorious frame the fullness of His life and strength, to the extent that these vessels of clay can hold it and use it for His service and glory.

It is apparent that the Holy Spirit has a direct
ministry for our bodies, even as Christ's body has a
direct relation to our physical being. Have we thus
received Him? Do we thus know Him? No longer
depending upon our natural strength, have we
learned the important secret, "He gives strength to
the weary and increases the power of the weak"
(Isaiah 40:29), "but those who hope in the LORD
will renew their strength. They will soar on wings
like eagles; they will run and not grow weary, they
will walk and not be faint" (40:31).

The Relation of the Holy Spirit to the Future Resurrection

This is the climax of the simple argument re-
specting the working of the Holy Spirit in our
bodies.

While He quickens our mortal bodies now,
there is awaiting us a glorious and immortal tabernacle which shall be fashioned like the body of
His glory.

Speaking of this, Paul says:

Now we know that if the earthly tent we
live in is destroyed, we have a building from
God, an eternal house in heaven, not built
by human hands. Meanwhile we groan,
longing to be clothed with our heavenly
dwelling, because when we are clothed, we
will not be found naked. For while we are in
this tent, we groan and are burdened, because we do not wish to be unclothed but to

be clothed with our heavenly dwelling, so that what is mortal may be swallowed up by life. Now it is God who has made us for this very purpose and has given us the Spirit as a deposit, guaranteeing what is to come. (2 Corinthians 5:1-5)

Anyone who knows the meaning of the word "earnest" need not have it demonstrated that it implies the first sample in actual kind of the flower and fruit which is to follow.

An earnest of the harvest is the first sheaf, the very same in kind as that which is to come. An earnest of the field purchased is a handful of the very soil which has been bought. And so, an earnest of the resurrection is a part of that resurrection life experienced now in our physical frame.

To say that the Holy Spirit in our hearts is the earnest would be to contradict the very meaning of the terms, to make a thing of a different class, an earnest of something utterly diverse. The Spirit in our hearts now is an earnest of our future spiritual exaltation. The Spirit in our mortal bodies now is an earnest of the resurrection of the body then in physical immortality.

This is exactly what Paul said in the parallel passage, Romans 8:23, "Not only so, but we ourselves, who have the firstfruits of the Spirit, groan inwardly as we wait eagerly for our adoption as sons, the redemption of our bodies."

We have the firstfruits of the resurrection and

we are waiting for the full harvest. The firstfruits
are: "And if the Spirit of him who raised Jesus
from the dead is living in you, he who raised
Christ from the dead will also give life to your
mortal bodies through his Spirit, who lives in
you" (8:11).

We have all we can hold in the vessel of clay
now; we shall then have all we can contain in the
larger vessel of glory when, thrilled with the rap-
turous touch of His life, we shall soar away from
the fetters of the tomb and the restraints of our
present frailties and limitations into all the might
and majesty of His own glorious life and power.
Then, like Him, our eyes shall be "like blazing
fire" and our feet "like bronze glowing in a fur-
nace" (Revelation 1:14-15). Our bodies will be
able to penetrate through material barriers, to rise
beyond the clouds, to spurn the restraining forces
of matter and nature, to possess immeasurable
space and share His own divine and mighty
works. For "when he appears, we shall be like
him, for we shall see him as he is" (1 John 3:2).

But this we may have even now in foretaste, as
the Spirit quickens our mortal bodies, until we
take hold of the glory of the resurrection.

How Shall We Walk in This Spirit of Life?

Initially, we must have Him as the occupant of
our heart; we must know Him by a deep and real
spiritual experience. Everything in its own order;
and the new order is, first, the spiritual and then
the material.

Like Him who came from the innermost shrine
of the tabernacle, moving outward to meet His people, so the Holy Spirit still comes from the holy
place of the heart until He fills all the extremities of
our physical being so that divine healing has been
called the overflow of the Holy Spirit from a heart
into every open channel of our physical life.

Next, we must distinctly recognize the promise
of His residence in our bodies and claim Him in
this specific way. Every new experience must first
be apprehended and then appropriated. We must
see it to be a redemption right and then put forth
our hand and take of the Tree of Life, eat and live
forever.

We must then receive the Holy Spirit as an
abiding guest into our flesh as well as our heart.
The word "dwell," in this verse, is a very strong
one. It is the Greek word *oikeo*, and in the last
clause the still stronger expression, *enoikeo*. It
means to dwell habitually; to dwell as we dwell at
home; to be the welcome, constant guest and find
His residence not only with us but, as the last
term expresses, in the innermost depths of our being.

Finally we must abide in Him by listening to
His voice, obeying His will, using our strength for
His service and glory and constantly recognizing
Him, and not mere natural strength, as the source
of our life.

This habit can be cultivated; God may have to
train us in it by cutting off the outward supplies
and sources of physical power. He may let the

natural life wither until it seems we must sink and die. Though, like Paul (2 Corinthians 4:11), we seem to be almost delivered unto death for Jesus' sake, yet we must receive the life of Christ in our mortal flesh, and we shall find that it is still as true as it was in Paran's desert and Judah's wilderness, that "Man does not live on bread alone, but on every word that comes from the mouth of God" (Matthew 4:4).

The Spirit of Comfort

. . . walking . . . in the comfort of the Holy Ghost. (Acts 9:31, KJV)

Our English translators have given to the Greek word "Paraclete," which the Lord Jesus applied to the Holy Spirit, the translation of "the Comforter." And while this term is not expressive of the complete sense of the original, yet it expresses very beautifully one of the most blessed characteristics and offices of the Holy Spirit.

The Spirit of Peace

He is the author of peace. It is a twofold peace: peace *with* God and peace *of* God. We find many references to this twofold rest. "Come to me, all you who are weary and burdened, and I will give you rest" (Matthew 11:28). This is the rest which the troubled soul receives when it comes to Christ for pardon. But then there is a deeper rest: "Take my yoke upon you and learn from me, for I am gentle and humble in heart, and you will find rest for your souls" (Matthew 11:29). This is experienced after the will is surrendered to God and the discipline of the Spirit is fully received. The prophet Isaiah announced, "You will keep in perfect peace him whose mind is steadfast, because he trusts in you" (Isaiah 26:3).

There is a deeper peace found in the salutation of the risen Savior when He came to the disciples in the Upper Room: "Peace be with you!" (John 20:21), He said, as He showed them His hands and His side. Later He breathed on them and added a second benediction of peace as they received the Holy Spirit. Peace with God is the effect of forgiveness, "Therefore, since we have been justified through faith, we have peace with God through our Lord Jesus Christ" (Romans 5:1). This is the gift of the Holy Spirit as He seals upon the heart the assurance of God's pardoning work and breathes the witness of acceptance.

This is, however, dependent upon our believing and resting in the promise. We must cooperate with the Holy Spirit. He witnesses "[h]aving believed, you were marked in him with a seal, the promised Holy Spirit" (Ephesians 1:13). "May the God of hope fill you with all joy and peace as you trust in him, so that you may overflow with hope by the power of the Holy Spirit" (Romans 15:13). These verses serve as scriptural evidence that we must cooperate in believing.

The peace of God is a deeper experience. It

comes from the indwelling of God Himself in the
heart that has been surrendered wholly to Him. It
is nothing less than the very heart of Christ resting
in our heart, possessing our spirit and imparting to
us the very same peace which He manifested
when, calm and victorious even in that awful hour
when all others were filled with dismay, He faced
the prospect of the garden and the cross. It is the
deep, tranquil, eternal rest of God taking the place
of the restless, troubled sea of our own thoughts,
fears and agitations. It is the very peace of God,
and it passes all understanding and keeps the heart
and mind through Christ Jesus our Lord. It is the
special gift of the Holy Spirit. Even more, it is His
own personal abiding, as the Dove of Rest, spread-
ing His wings over the troubled sea of human
strife and passion and bringing His own everlasting rest.

Have we entered into His rest? Are we walking with Him in the secret place of the Most
High? What gift is more necessary and delightful in this world of disquiet and change? What
would the world not give for an opiate that
could charm away its cares and fears and lull its
heart to such divine repose. Yet men turn from
the Paraclete of love and refuse to take the gift
for which their hearts are breaking, and their
lives are wearing out in the fret and friction of
strife and sin. This is the true element of spiritual growth and power. "In quietness and trust
is your strength" (Isaiah 30:15). To make this a
reality is the mission of the Comforter. "There-

fore, since the promise of entering his rest still stands, let us be careful that none of you be found to have fallen short of it" (Hebrews 4:1). "Let us, therefore, make every effort to enter that rest, so that no one will fall by following their example of disobedience" (4:11).

2   ## The Spirit of Joy

This is a deeper and fuller spring, but the source is the same—the heart of the Comforter. The kingdom of God, we are told, is not meat and drink, but righteousness, peace and joy in the Holy Spirit. This also is the joy of Christ Himself. It is the Spirit's business to take the things that are Christ's and reveal them to us. The Master has said, "I have told you this so that my joy may be in you and that your joy may be complete" (John 15:11). "Until now you have not asked for anything in my name. Ask and you will receive, and your joy will be complete" (16:24).

We have some conception of His joy. In the dark and dreadful hour when the powers of darkness were gathering about Him for the final struggle, and even His Father's face was about to be covered with the awful cloud of desertion and judgment, still He could rise above His surroundings and troubles and give to His followers the words of encouragement—"Do not let your hearts be troubled" (John 14:1).

Like the martyrs afterward—at the stake and amid the flames—who testified that so deep was their inward joy that they were unconscious of external agony, so Christ was transported above His anguish by the very joy of His Father's presence and love. It was this that enabled Him to endure, "for the joy set before him endured the cross, scorning its shame" (Hebrews 12:2). He did not see the deep, dark valley of humiliation, but the heights of resurrection life and ascension glory just beyond. He was lifted above the consciousness of the present by the vision of hope and the joy of the Lord. This is the joy He will give to us. It is nothing less than the fullness of His own heart, throbbing in our being and sharing with us His own immutable blessedness.

Therefore, this joy is wholly independent of surrounding circumstances or natural temperament. It is not a spirit of native cheerfulness, but it is a perennial fountain of divine gladness, springing up from sources that lie far below the soil of human nature. It is the same anointing of which the prophet said to Christ, "God, your God, has set you above your companions by anointing you with the oil of joy" (Hebrews 1:9).

Now this divine joy is the privilege of all consecrated believers. We need it for victory in the trying places of life. "[T]he joy of the LORD is your strength" (Nehemiah 8:10). Satan always takes special advantage of a depressed and discouraged heart. Victory must be won in the conflict by a spirit of gladness and praise. The hosts of God must march into the battle with songs of rejoicing. The world must see the light of heaven in our faces if it would believe in the reality of our religion.

Therefore, the Scriptures exhort us, "Rejoice in the Lord always" (Philippians 4:4) and, "[G]ive thanks in all circumstances, for this is God's will for you in Christ Jesus" (1 Thessalonians 5:18). The secret of such a love must be a heart possessed and overflowing with the Holy Spirit. "But the fruit of the Spirit is love, joy, peace" (Galatians 5:22). We cannot find these springs in the soil of time; they flow from the throne of God and of the Lamb. But the one who dwells in the innermost shrine of the Master's presence will know it and reflect it. It can no more be concealed than the sunlight, and it will light up the humblest life and the most trying situation, just as the sun shines through the dark vault, if only it can find an opening where it may enter in. Are you walking in the light of the Lord and filled with His joy? Can you sing:

> God is the treasure of my soul,
>   A source of lasting joy;
> A joy which want cannot impair
>   Nor death itself destroy?

3. *The Spirit of Comfort and Consolation*

It is especially in the hour of distress and trial that the Comforter becomes manifest in His peculiar ministry of consolation and love. It is then that the promise is fulfilled which applies more especially to this person of the Godhead as the very Mother of the soul. "As a mother comforts her child, so will I comfort you; and you will be comforted over Jerusalem" (Isaiah 66:13).

Comfort implies the existence of trial. The happiest life is not the one freest from affliction; rather, they who walk in the Spirit will always be familiar with the paths of sorrow and the adverse circumstances of life. Nowhere are the followers of the Man of Sorrows promised exemption from the fellowship of His sufferings, but every element of blessing they possess carries with it an added source of trial. To them the world is less a home than to its own children, and their dearest friends are the readiest to misunderstand their lives and cross their wishes. To them comes the experience of temptation and spiritual conflict, as it does not come to the worldling and the sinner, and they have often cause to feel and know

> The path of sorrow and that path alone,
>   Leads to the land where sorrow is unknown.
> No traveler ever reached that blessed abode,
>   Who found not thorns and briers in the road.

But all these are but occasions to prove the love and faithfulness of God. The storm cloud provides the background for the rainbow; the falling tear gives occasion for the gentle hand of the Comforter to wipe it away.

The comfort is in proportion to the trial. There is a certain balance of joy and sorrow. As the sufferings of Christ abound in us, so our consolation also abounds in Christ. As far as the pendulum swings backward, so far it swings forward. Every trial is, therefore, a prophecy of blessing to the one who walks with Jesus.

A saint of God remarked, near the close of life, "God has seemed all my life to be so sorry for the trials He gave me in the beginning, that He has been trying to make up for it ever since." This is a blessed compensation even here, and by-and-by we shall find that "our light and momentary troubles are achieving for us an eternal glory that far outweighs them all" (2 Corinthians 4:17).

Times of trial are, therefore, often our times of greatest joy. God's nightingales sing at midnight, and

> Sorrow touched by God grows bright
>   With more than rapturous ray,
> As darkness shows us worlds of light
>   We never saw by day.

It was when the apostles were turned out of Antioch by a mob of respectable men and honorable women that the record was added. "And the disciples were filled with joy and with the Holy Spirit" (Acts 13:52). It was when the fig tree refused to blossom, the vines were stripped of their accustomed fruit and nature was robed in the graveclothes of death that Habakkuk's song rose to its highest notes of triumph and he could say, "[Y]et I will rejoice in the LORD, I will be joyful in God my Savior" (Habakkuk 3:18). There is such a thing as being "sorrowful, yet always rejoicing" (2 Corinthians 6:10); a bittersweet which draws its quintessence of joy from the very wormwood and the gall, and which knows not whether to weep or sing as it cries with Pascal, in the one breath "joy upon joy, tears upon tears!"

What a wonderful testimony to the grace of God and the Spirit's abundant love when we can rise above our circumstances and "[c]onsider it pure joy, my brothers, whenever you face trials of many kinds" (James 1:2), and "rejoice that you participate in the sufferings of Christ, so that you may be overjoyed when his glory is revealed" (1 Peter 4:13).

If we would know the full comfort of the Holy Spirit we must cooperate with Him and rejoice by simple faith, often when our circumstances are all forbidding and even our feelings give no response of sympathy or conscious joy. It is a great thing to learn to *count it* all joy. Counting is not the language of poetry or sentiment but of cold, unerring calculation. It adds up the column thus: sorrow, temptation, difficulty, opposition, depression, desertion, danger, discouragement on every side, but at the bottom of the column God's presence, God's will, God's joy, God's promise, God's recompense. "For our light and momentary troubles are achieving for us an eternal glory that far outweighs them all" (2 Corinthians 4:17). How much does the column amount to? The sum of all the addition is ALL JOY, for "I consider that our present sufferings are not worth comparing with the glory that will be revealed in us" (Romans 8:18).

That is the way to count your joy. Singly, a

given circumstance may not seem joyful, but counted in with God and His presence and promise it makes a glorious sum in the arithmetic of faith. We can rejoice in the Lord as an act of will, and when we do, the Comforter will soon bring all our emotions into line—yes, and our circumstances too. Paul said it very well: "I rejoice. Yes, and I will continue to rejoice" (Philippians 1:18).

The Holy Spirit's joys and consolations are administered to the heart in His infinite and sovereign wisdom according to His purpose for our spiritual training, and with reference to our spiritual state or our immediate needs and prospects. Frequently, He sends His sweetest whispers as the reward of special obedience in some difficult and trying place. Not only at the judgment, but now also does the Master say, "Well done, good and faithful servant! . . . Come and share your master's happiness" (Matthew 25:21). That joy is experienced here, and the good and faithful servant has the recompense of special service and obedience in the place of difficulty and testing.

Sometimes the Spirit's comforts are sent to prepare us for some impending trial, in order that when the storm bursts upon us we may remember the Savior's love and be cheered and sustained through the trying hour, just as the Holy Spirit came and the Father's voice was heard on Jordan's banks prior to the 40 days of fierce temptation.

At times the Spirit's comfort may come just after some dark and terrible conflict, even as the angels appeared after Gethsemane to comfort our weary and suffering Lord. Sometimes, also, His comforts are withdrawn to keep us from leaning too strongly on sensible joys, and to discipline us in the life of simple faith and teach us to trust when we cannot see the face of our Beloved, or hear His voice.

We must always remember, in connection with our varied experiences, that even comfort and joy are not to be the aim and goal of our hearts. The principle of our Christian life is simple faith, and our purpose, faithful obedience and service to our Master.

> Not enjoyment and not sorrow
>   Is our destined end and way;
> But to act that each tomorrow
>   Finds us farther than today.

The life that is naturally influenced by sunshine or shadow will be ephemeral and will change its hue, like the chameleon, with the seasons and surroundings. Indeed, the real source of lasting joy is to ignore our own emotions and feelings and act uniformly on the twin principles of faith and duty. Many people try to obtain joyful emotions just as they would buy cut flowers in winter. They are bright and fragrant for a few hours, but they have no root and they wither away with the sunset. Far better and wiser to plant the root in the fertile ground, to water it and to wait for it. In a little while the lasting blossoms will open their petals and breathe out their fragrance on the air. So the joy that springs from trust and permanent spiritual life is as abiding as its source.

Let us, therefore, learn to ignore the immediate impressions that lie upon the surface of our consciousness and steadfastly walk in the fellowship and will of the divine Spirit. Then there shall grow in our hearts and lives the roots of happiness and all the fruits of joy and consolation.

God often has to withdraw, for a time, the conscious joy that He may prove us and develop in us the faith that trusts Him and loves Him for Himself rather than for His gifts.

A friend once came to us complaining that her spiritual joy had left and that her heart was like a stone. There seemed to be no disobedience in her life and no defect in her faith, and we could only commit her to the Lord for the teaching she might need. Later she came, her face radiant, to tell what had happened. "The darkness," she said, "continued until I told the Lord that if He wanted me to be willing to trust Him in the dark, and to bear this for Him, I would do so as long as He was pleased to continue it. The moment I had yielded my will and accepted His, the light returned, far brighter than before, and I knew that He had only been testing me to teach me to trust Him for His own sake, and to walk by faith and not by sight."

Let us delight ourselves in the Lord, and He will give us the desires of our heart. Let us aim supremely to please and glorify Him. To do so is to find that "to glorify God" is "to enjoy Him forever." If we will rise above even the joy of the

Lord to the Lord Himself, the Word tells us, "I will see you again and you will rejoice, and no one will take away your joy" (John 16:22), "that my joy may be in you and that your joy may be complete" (John 15:11). "Your sun will never set again, and your moon will wane no more; the LORD will be your everlasting light, and your days of sorrow will end" (Isaiah 60:20).

The Spirit of Love

[L]ive a life of love. (Ephesians 5:2)
But the fruit of the Spirit is love. (Galatians 5:22)

The legend has come to us that when the apostle John was old and waiting for his Master's call, he used to come to the pulpit of the church in Ephesus each Lord's Day, look tenderly into the faces of the people and simply say, "Little children, love one another," and sit down. When asked why he said nothing else, he answered, "There is nothing else to say; that is all there is, for '[w]hoever lives in love lives in God, and God in him'" (1 John 4:16).

Certainly, both Christ and His apostles have given to love at least the supreme, if not the exclusive, place in the circle of Christian graces. Love was the new commandment which Christ left with His disciples, and to which John refers in

First John when he says, "And this is his command: to believe in the name of his Son, Jesus Christ, and to love one another as he commanded us" (1 John 3:23). Paul also declares, "[L]ove is the fulfillment of the law" (Romans 13:10). And Christ Himself has declared that the whole law is fulfilled in one word—even in this: "Love your neighbor as yourself" (Romans 13:9).

Someone has beautifully analyzed the fruit of the Spirit in Galatians 5:22-23 and shown that all the graces mentioned there are but various forms of love itself. The writer is not speaking of different fruits but of one fruit, the fruit of the Spirit, and the various words that follow are but phases and descriptions of the one fruit, which is love itself. *Joy,* which is first mentioned, is love on wings; *peace,* which follows, is love folding its wings and nestling under the wings of God; *longsuffering* is love enduring; *gentleness* is love in society; *goodness* is love in action; *faith* is love confiding; *meekness* is love stooping; *temperance* is true self-love and the proper regard for our own real interests, which is as much the duty of love as is regard for the interests of others. Thus we see that love is essential to our whole Christian character—indeed it is the complement and crown of all else.

In the catalog of spiritual gifts described by Paul in First Corinthians, it is named as preeminent to all the gifts of power, and the more excellent way, better than any enduement even of miraculous working or transcendent wisdom, without which all else will make us but as "a resounding gong or a clanging cymbal" (1 Corinthians 13:1).

In the book of Colossians Paul describes the investiture of holy character. After our old garments have been laid aside and the new robes put on, we are instructed to put on, over all the rest, love, which is the "perfect bond." Love is the girdle that holds all the other garments in place and keeps them from falling off. So, the soul without love must lose even the chief advantage of all other gifts, and his faith and service will be rendered ineffectual for lack of love. It is the chief ministry of the Holy Spirit to teach us this critical lesson.

We must learn from Him that love is not a natural quality but a direct gift of divine grace. The very word for love is charity, or *caritas*, and this is derived from the root *charis*, or grace. The primary idea conveyed by the Bible term for love is that it is a gift and not a natural quality. There is much earthborn love, and it would be narrow and blind to ignore the human virtues which are recorded all through history. The love of a mother for her child, the tender affection of the husband and wife, the brother and friend, the devotion of the patriot to his country and the many positive aspects of the human character—these are holy affections which we would not and do not need to ignore. But human love has its limitations.

The love which the Holy Spirit teaches is not confined to any class or condition. Like the love of God Himself it is able to reach and embrace not only the stranger and the alien, but the unworthy, the unlovely, the unloving and even the most malignant enemy and the most uncongenial object. It is nothing less than the very heart of God Himself infused into our heart, imparted to us through the Holy Spirit. We cannot wring it out of our selfish hearts or work it up by any effort of our will. It must come down to us from the very heart of God and be shed abroad by the Holy Spirit Himself. This delightful fact makes the exercise of love a possibility for even the coldest and hardest heart. If it is a gift of grace, then it is available for all, and we only have to realize our need, yield ourselves unreservedly to God, be willing to receive it and exercise it and go forth to fulfill it in His strength. Because it is a gift, it involves no merit on the part of the receiver, for it is not our love but the grace of our Lord Jesus Christ, to whom must ever be all the glory.

The love of God must be founded, like every other spiritual grace, on the exercise of faith. The apostle John, who understood this subject better than any other, gives the simple philosophy of love in these words, "We love because he first loved us" (1 John 4:19); "And so we know and rely on the love God has for us" (4:16). We must believe without wavering in God's personal love to us before we can love Him in return. A single doubt in the heart concerning this will cloud the whole heavens. The spirit of implicit confidence in God will always lead to a spirit of filial love. If we love Him who begets, we shall also love them that are begotten of Him.

Faith is, indeed, the channel of all spiritual blessing. Peter said, "[A]dd to your faith goodness; and to goodness, knowledge; and to knowledge, self-control" (2 Peter 1:5-6). Also, the apostles, when Christ was urgently instructing them concerning the height and depth to which the forgiveness of injuries should extend, exclaimed to the Lord, "Increase our faith!" (Luke 17:5). They did not say, "Increase our love," for they seemed to have learned that if they had the faith which they should possess, they would inevitably possess the love. This is true. The fountain of love will always spring to the same height as the headwaters of faith have reached.

In order to receive this heavenly gift, the soul must be wholly surrendered to Christ and receive the Holy Spirit as an abiding presence to bring into the heart the life of Jesus Christ, and to write the law of love upon the heart, according to the terms of the new covenant. "I will put my laws in their minds and write them on their hearts" (Hebrews 8:10) is the promise of this new covenant. This law is nothing but love, for love is the substance of the law, and the Holy Spirit came on the day of Pentecost as the spirit of power and obedience.

We enter into this new covenant, therefore, when we receive the Holy Spirit as our personal life and indwelling guide and strength. He brings into our spirit the abiding presence of Jesus Christ, uniting us to His person in such an intimate and perfect manner that we receive His very life into our own; we love in His love, and live in His very being. In order to do this there must, of course, be a renunciation of our own life and will and the complete consecration of ourselves to Him. Then we receive Christ to abide, and all our life from this point is through the virtue of His abiding union with us. This is the true secret of divine love.

A distinguished French evangelist was converted to God by preaching on the text, "Love the Lord your God with all your heart and with all your soul and with all your mind and with all your strength" (Mark 12:30). Finding as he preached his own inability to meet the demands of love, he was forced to fall back upon the Lord Jesus Christ to meet his helplessness. He publicly acknowledged to the people that there was one way alone through which he could have help to obey this supreme law—the grace of the Lord Jesus Christ. In short, the secret of love is the same as all other graces: "I no longer live, but Christ lives in me" (Galatians 2:20). This is what He is waiting to do for every willing heart.

But it is in the exercise of love in our practical Christian life that our chief lessons in walking with the Spirit must be learned. Our heavenly Teacher leads us in detail through the blessed yet often painful discipline of the school of experience and grounds us not only in the principles, but in the most difficult practice of this heavenly grace. One of His most frequent leadings is to bring us into a situation where we are required to exercise a love which we do not really possess. We are confronted with circumstances which severely test our spirits.

Perhaps some unkindness is done to us, or we are associated with uncongenial and disagreeable persons. Or we hear of some trial that someone whom we dislike is facing, and we are strongly tempted to conclude that they deserve the affliction and are only suffering judgment which they have brought upon themselves. The Holy Spirit would teach us not to judge them at all, or even think in terms of condemnation but rather pray for them and thus secure our victory of love.

Humanly speaking, it is not in us to do this; our selfishness or pride leaps to the front, passes its judgment, recoils from the uncongenial touch, is tempted to take pleasure in their calamity. At the same time, we are intensely conscious of condemnation and humiliation because of this ignominious failure in the grace of love. We see the divine standard: "Charity suffereth long, and is kind" (1 Corinthians 13:4, KJV). Charity makes no account of the evil, charity is not provoked, bears all things, believes all things, hopes all things, endures all things. And we are conscious of our inability to meet it. There is a painful conflict, perhaps a struggle with self and the stronger uprising of the old spirit of prejudice and malice; and then the cry, "What a wretched man I am! Who will rescue me?" (Romans 7:24).

It is at this point that Christ is revealed to us as the Source of victory and the Spirit of love. As we look from our hearts to Him and cling to Him in our helplessness, we find His love sufficient, and the heart is quieted and filled with His thoughts,

His gentleness, His divine forbearance, His forgiveness, meekness and patience. We are "strengthened . . . according to his glorious might so that you may have great endurance and patience" (Colossians 1:11).

It often seems very strange to those who have just yielded themselves to God that they should be immediately thrown into circumstances more trying than they have ever experienced, and every right thing they try to do seems harder than before. But this is just God's way of impressing the lesson upon us, showing us our need and throwing us upon His power and grace. When we have learned the lesson, the difficulty is removed or made easier.

It is a good thing to recognize in our trials not so much obstacles that have come to overwhelm us as teachers that have met us on our way to bring us deeper lessons and greater blessings.

Another way by which the Spirit teaches us the exercise of love is by showing us God's thoughts about us and teaching us to see persons as He sees them, not so much in their present character or personal unworthiness as in their relation to Christ—especially in the light of what His grace is working in them and is going to finally develop in their character. God looks at us not as we are but as we are to Christ. He loves us not for our sake but for Christ's sake and for His own sake. He loves us because of something in Himself which cannot help loving even the unlovely. God always looks beyond our present to the future ideal which

His love has for us and to which it is bringing us. God sees us, not as we are today, but as we shall be when He has accomplished the purpose of His grace in us. Then we shall shine forth as the sun in the kingdom of our Father.

Let us, like Him, look at others, not in the present, but in the light of the glorious future. We should love them as He loves them, and be lifted above all that is trying and into the victory of faith and love. If we truly believe in God's purpose of grace for us, we must believe likewise for others.

There is nothing more beautiful than this spirit in God Himself, which refuses to recognize the faults of His children. He said, "Surely they are my people, sons who will not be false to me" (Isaiah 63:8). He was not willing to see their faults and sins. It was the blindness of love; the blessed blindness which He would teach us also, and in which we find our choicest victories and lose most of our burdens.

There is a parable of a man who met a traveler on the road, dragged down almost to the earth by an unequal burden which he carried on his shoulders—one hanging in front, the other behind. The one hanging in front contained the bad deeds of his neighbors. It was so full that his head was bowed almost to the ground, while the odor that came from the offensive mass almost suffocated him. The sack carried behind contained their good deeds. It seemed almost empty and would not balance the overwhelming weight of the other.

While the man tried to persuade him to reverse

the load, another traveler came up to them walking lightly, head erect, face shining. He, too, had two sacks on his back, but they did not seem to oppress, but rather to rest him. The one in front contained the good deeds of his neighbors. He never seemed to tire of contemplating this particular burden which, he said, instead of weighing him down seemed to pull him forward on his journey.

When the gentleman asked him what he carried in the other sack, he said, "Oh, that is where I keep the bad actions of my friends." "But," said the other, "I don't see any there." "Well," said the traveler, "I have made a little hole in the bottom of the bag. When anything disagreeable occurs I just pitch it over my shoulder in the sack and it drops out at the bottom. So I have nothing to hold me back and my journey is very delightful and easy."

The greatest value of love is the blessing it brings to us. The heaviest curse of hate is the corrosion it leaves on the heart. Every time a temptation comes to harshly judge another or take pleasure in his calamity, and we pray for him instead, we have obtained a blessing far richer than his. Every time we linger on an injury or harbor an ungracious spirit, we have depleted our spiritual strength in proportion. Love is not only duty, it is also life, and selfishness is self-destruction. There is no greater truth than this: "The man who loves his life will lose it, while the man who hates his life in this world will keep it for eternal life" (John 12:25).

While it is true that the Holy Spirit will always give us the victory and grace of love, yet we have a more solemn part to perform; we must be willing to choose it. This is often the very crisis of defeat. Pride and bitterness are not willing even to receive the love of God. Some would rather have their revenge than their victory; they would not forgive even if they could, and the Lord lets them have their way and their sin becomes its own avenger.

We have occasionally met even Christians who do not want to love certain people but rather take real pleasure in disliking them. There have been times when those who have struggled for this grace of love have asked, "Why is it God does not give me love?" We have questioned, "Do you really want it? Do you really choose to love some persons? Would you be glad at this moment to be able to treat them with all sincerity and kindness?" They have looked into their hearts and honestly replied, "I do not believe I am really willing." In that moment they have felt they did not really want this blessing; therefore, they did not have it.

Do you find yourself in this state? If so, pause and remember with deep solemnity your earliest and simplest prayer, "Forgive us our trespasses as we forgive them that trespass against us." There are two inexcusable sins: One is the unbelief that rejects Christ; the other is the bitterness that refuses to love one's brother. He who died for His enemies has said, "But if you do not forgive men their sins, your Father will not forgive your sins" (Matthew 6:15). It is vain to say we cannot love; He knows we cannot, but He is willing to give us the love if we are honestly willing to receive it. Because of this we are without excuse.

There are many lessons in the school of love into which we shall be led as we walk in the Spirit day by day. We shall find the love of God Himself shed abroad in our heart and our love to Him kept alive and continually quickened in an ever-burning fire. It will not always be emotion, but it will be the purpose of obedience which is the truest test of love, for He has said, "If you love me, you will obey what I command" (John 14:15). And we shall find it utterly His love, not our own. We need not guard it like some transient and uncertain feeling which we are always afraid of losing. Indeed, it will possess us as a divine principle, springing up when needed like a well of water whose fountains are in the very heart of Christ. It will be the love of Christ Himself to the Father, living and working in our hearts.

We will find our natural affections intensified, and that we can love our friends more fervently than before, yet more restfully, more purely— more for His sake and glory and less for their sakes and our own.

We shall find our Christian ties divinely quickened. We shall understand the language of the Bible when it speaks of Christian fellowship and unity. Our hearts shall be knit together in love and we shall know what Paul meant when he spoke of the consolation in Christ, the fellowship of the Spirit, the bowels of mercies, the mutual love of Christ's disciples. It shall then be true that the ties of spiritual relationship seem more intense than any bonds of human affection.

Our love for souls shall also be divinely imparted and sustained. Men and women will be laid upon our hearts and we shall long over them with an intensity of desire to which there is no parallel in human nature or experience. It will be a luxury of joy to labor for them, minister to them and suffer for their sake. If we are required to spend our lives in the very cesspools of iniquity we shall not feel the hideous surroundings. Though called to serve in areas crowded with poverty and sin, the air fetid with foul breath, soiled clothing and moral pollution, they shall seem to us like the gate of heaven. Joy will give radiance to our face and wings to our feet in the errands of ministering love. No task will seem trying, no sinner unattractive, to one whose heart has been thus possessed with the Savior's heart of love.

Love will make a mother bear for her child humiliating drudgeries and excruciating agonies which no servile wages could bribe her to endure. Love for souls will give zest, freshness and perpetual delight to all ministry. "So I was [taken] home to prison," wrote the quaint John Bunyan of the place that the love of God had made a paradise. "I wrote because joy did make me write," was his explanation of the book that has charmed many generations. Only such service for Christ will sustain us through the toils and sacrifices, the fields of wretchedness and sin. This love the Holy Spirit alone can give, and He will freely give it to every consecrated heart that receives Him fully.

This is but the spirit of His own ministry. For more than 1,900 years the Holy Spirit has dwelt in a hospital of moral leprosy and contagion. Nothing could have held Him in such scenes of sin and repulsion but love stronger than anything that mortals know. This earth has been His chosen home and the heart of sinful men His willing abode. He will shed abroad the same love in every heart that receives Him.

Beloved, shall we open all our being to His heavenly power and enter into all the fullness of the love of God? This is the divine nature; this is the substance of heaven; this is the essence of all enduring holiness and happiness. This is what the Holy Spirit longs to teach every willing disciple. Let us receive Him and walk in Him, and so "live a life of love" (Ephesians 5:2).

The Spirit of Power

But you will receive power when the Holy Spirit comes on you. (Acts 1:8)

The world is discovering, even in the scientific field, that power is not to be measured by mere mechanical and material forces. There was a time when the strength of an army could be estimated by the numbers and the fighting qualities of its soldiers, but today a small battery of artillery could destroy an entire phalanx of Nebuchadnezzar's, Alexander's or Caesar's army.

The walls of Babylon would not stand against the mines and missiles of modern military science. The power of a sunbeam is stronger than the momentum of an iceberg. A single jet of gas will move the mechanism of machinery, and we are beginning to understand the great fundamental force of electricity, which will perhaps ultimately be proved to be the principal form of material force in the natural universe. Of course, we know that power belongs to God, and that the Holy Spirit, the executive of the Trinity, is the dispenser and agent of divine power.

Our departing Lord said, "You will receive power when the Holy Spirit comes on you" (Acts 1:8). He is the personal power, and as we receive Him we are empowered for all His will and work.

Let us first consider the nature of true spiritual power. It is not intellectual force. There is force in the human mind. Man can move his fellowman by eloquence and persuasion and can overcome the forces of matter by his ingenuity and skill, but this is not the power that the Holy Spirit gives us for the work of Christ. Often it is a hindrance to His effectual working, and it is not until our confidence in our own thoughts and reasonings has been renounced that He can use "the foolish things of the world to shame the wise; . . . the weak things of the world to shame the strong. . . . [S]o that no one may boast before him" (1 Corinthians 1:27, 29).

The power by which the orator sways his audience, producing deep emotion and enthusiasm, is not the power of the Holy Spirit. The same effect may be produced by delightful music or splendid acting, and the tears of the sanctuary may be no holier than those of the opera or the theatre. Even the most logical presentation of divine things, which delights the hearers and impresses the imagination and the understanding, may be utterly destitute of real spiritual power. Some of the most outstanding preachers of the past two centuries preached with little definite spiritual results in the known conversion of souls.

It is not mere truth as truth that produces spiritual results, but it is the power of God accompanying it through the Holy Spirit.

True spiritual power is not the power of organization or numbers. Much of the power of Christianity today is the natural result of organized forces. Many a successful church owes its prosperity, in a great measure, to the business principles on which it is run. Its influence is made up largely of the social elements which constitute it, the numbers which attend it or the effective machinery by which it is moved. But this may involve no spiritual power whatever.

It is not inconsistent with spiritual power; the Holy Spirit may work in the channels of order and systematic work, but all of this may exist in the most complete form and yet it be simply a religious club and ecclesiastical machinery.

A minister may build up his church just as a man builds up his business, and the ambition which accomplishes his splendid ideal may be of precisely the same kind as that which has founded and developed the great financial enterprises of our age. There is no more perfect an organization in the world than Romanism. Its machinery is superb, but it knows nothing of spiritual power.

In *The Rhyme of the Ancient Mariner*, Coleridge has drawn the picture of a ship of death drifting across the ocean, manned by lifeless forms of men—a dead man at the helm, a dead man in the rigging, a dead man on the bridge, a dead man on the deck, drifting in silence across the deep. Someone has represented a formal church as a ship of death, with all the forms of life, but without *the* life; a dead man in the pulpit and dead souls in the pews, while the voice of heaven sadly complains, "[Y]ou have a reputation of being alive, but you are dead" (Revelation 3:1).

Some writers are very fond of quoting statistics of Christianity and speaking of the four or five hundred millions who today are under Christian governments, so-called, and the more than three hundred millions who are nominally Christians. If we were to deduct from these figures the numbers who belong to the Papal church and then the members of national Protestant establishments which do not even profess to admit members on the ground of conversion, there would be a frightful deduction, and a very small remnant who might even be claimed as genuine Christians.

How many would be left who would admit that they knew nothing of the power of the Holy Spirit? Spiritual power may operate without any organized basis. Like the torrent, it can break through the banks and barriers and sweep over the church of God regardless of its forms and formalities.

In our day God has been pleased to give it, in the most eminent degree, to the men and women who are not even members of the formal circle of the ordained ministry, but have been chosen by God partly because they represented none of the elements which are usually connected with power. We can have this power under any circumstances, and the feeblest church, the most isolated worker, the least influential minister of Christ, may become an instrument of blessing to the whole church of God.

What Is Spiritual Power?

It is the power which convicts of sin. It is the power that makes the hearers see themselves as God sees them and humbles them in the dust. It sends people home from the house of God not feeling better, but worse; not always admiring the preacher, but often so tried that they perhaps resolve that they will never hear him again. Still, they know in their inmost soul that he is right and they are wrong. It is the power of conviction; the power that awakens the conscience and says to the soul, "You are the man!" (2 Samuel 12:7); it is the power of which the apostle Paul speaks in connection with his own ministry, "by setting forth the truth plainly we commend ourselves to every man's conscience in the sight of God" (2 Corinthians 4:2).

They who possess this power will not always be popular preachers, but they will always be effectual workers. Sometimes the hearer will almost think that they are being personal, and that someone has disclosed to them his secret sins. Speaking of such a sermon, one of our most honored evan-

gelists said that he felt so indignant with the
preacher under whom he was converted that he
waited for some time near the door for the purpose of giving him a beating for daring to expose
him in the way he had done, thinking that some-
body had informed on him.

Let us covet this power. It is the very stamp and
seal of the Holy Spirit on a faithful minister.

After some of Mr. Moody's evangelistic meet-
ings, it is said that thousands and thousands of
dollars were returned anonymously, or otherwise,
to the original owners. Men's consciences had
been awakened; the power of God had arraigned
them before the bar of justice.

Spiritual power is the power that lifts up Christ
and makes Him real to the apprehension of the
hearer. Some sermons leave upon the mind a vivid
impression of the truth; others leave upon the
mind the picture of the Savior. It is not so much
an idea as a person. This is true preaching, and
this is the Holy Spirit's most blessed and congenial ministry. He loves to draw in heavenly lines
the face of Jesus and make Him shine out over
every page of the Bible and every paragraph of the
sermon as a face of beauty and a heart of love.

Let us cultivate this power, for this is what the
struggling, hungry world wants—to know its Savior. "We would like to see Jesus" (John 12:21) is
still its cry, and the answer still is, "I, when I am
lifted up from the earth, will draw all men to myself" (John 12:32).

Spiritual power is the power that leads men to a

decision. It is not merely that they know something they did not know before, that they get new thoughts and conceptions of truth which they carry away to remember and reflect upon, or even that they feel the deepest and most stirring emotions of religious feeling. It is the power of the Spirit that presses them to action—prompt, decisive, positive action.

This is the best test of power. It was the test of ancient eloquence; it was the glory of Demosthenes that while under the eloquence of other orators the multitudes hurrahed for the speaker; under his matchless tongue they forgot all about Demosthenes and shouted with one voice, "Let us go and fight Philip."

The power of the Holy Spirit leads men to decide for God and to enlist against Satan, to give up habits of sin and to make great and everlasting decisions.

The Lord desires to speak in His name, in demonstration of the Spirit and power, that the result shall be, as Paul himself expresses it on writing to the Thessalonians, "[O]ur gospel came to you not simply with words, but also with power" (1 Thessalonians 1:5), and "[Y]ou turned to God from idols to serve the living and true God, and to wait for his Son from heaven, . . . Jesus, who rescues us from the coming wrath" (1 Thessalonians 1:9-10).

The Elements and Sources of Power

It is the power of Christ. It is His own personal working both in the worker and upon the hearers.

"All authority," He says, "in heaven and on earth has been given to me. . . . And surely I am with you always, to the very end of the age" (Matthew 28:18-20).

Power is not given unto us, but unto Him, and we are constantly to recognize His living and perpetual presence and to count upon His direct working. If, therefore, we would have this power, we must be personally united to Him and have Him as an abiding presence. God does not want to glorify us and to show to the world our importance, but to glorify His Son Jesus Christ and hold up His power and glory.

It is the power of the Holy Spirit. He is the agent who reveals Christ and manifests His mighty working. Therefore, the power is directly connected with the Spirit personally, in the very promise of Christ concerning the Comforter. "When he comes, he will convict the world of guilt in regard to sin and righteousness and judgment" (John 16:8). It is not said that we shall convict, but that He shall convict, operating both in the worker and the hearer's heart.

Again, in the promise of Christ just before His ascension, it is said, "But you will receive power when the Holy Spirit comes on you" (Acts 1:8). It is not power *through* the Holy Spirit, but it is the very power *of* the personal Holy Spirit.

In the account of the gifts of the Spirit (1 Corinthians 12) that were to remain in the New Testament church, all are directly connected with the personal working of the Holy Spirit: "to another faith by the same Spirit, . . . to another miraculous powers" (12:9-10); but, in order that the power should not be connected with the individual in any undue personal sense, it is added, "All these are the work of one and the same Spirit, and he gives them to each one, just as he determines" (12:11).

The history of the Christian church has no more striking feature—or less—than that connected with the phenomena of the Spirit of power. All that have been mightily used of God in the conversion of souls and the building up of the kingdom of Christ have recognized His personal baptism as the secret of their power. It was after He had come upon Peter at Pentecost that 3,000 souls were converted by a very simple message. It was His fiery truth that made George Whitefield the power of God unto the salvation of innumerable thousands. It was He who fell upon Charles Finney and his audiences and so filled whole towns with the divine Presence that the hands in the factories would fall down at their work and begin to plead for mercy. It is to the day when He fell upon an illiterate Sunday school worker on the public streets, until he wept for holy joy, that Dwight Moody traces back all his unparalleled usefulness. Many a lowlier worker could tell of a similar story of weakness changed to might and ignorance made into a channel of divine teaching and blessing through the power of the Holy Spirit in a consecrated heart and life.

Let us honor Him as the personal source of all

spiritual power, and He will surely honor us. He holds the key to every human heart. He is the source of the highest thought and the truest feeling. He has given to us equipment for our holy ministry for Christ, and we may boldly claim His all-sufficient power and presence.

It is the power of truth. When united to Christ and accompanied by the Holy Spirit, the gospel is the power of God unto salvation. Apart from the Spirit it is only "the letter [that] kills" (2 Corinthians 3:6), but accompanied by the Holy Spirit it is wonderfully and divinely adapted to convict of sin, to lead to Christ and to establish the foundations of faith—hope, love and holy character. It is not the way we present the gospel, but it is the pure and simple gospel itself which is the power of God. It is the fundamental elements of the gospel, especially the glorious truth that Christ has died for our sins and brought in an everlasting righteousness and salvation by His resurrection and intercession.

It is wonderful how God often uses the plain statement of the gospel for the salvation of souls. The sermons of Peter and Paul in the Acts of the Apostles are destitute of either logic or rhetoric. They are simply statements of the great fact that Christ had died and risen to save men, and that by simply accepting this message we are saved. It does indeed seem foolish in its weakness, and yet again and again God has shown that it has the power to change the human heart as nothing else has. How stupendous its result at Pentecost when thousands were saved under the simple proclamation! How marvelous its fruits wherever Paul proclaimed it, not with wisdom of words, but purposely in great simplicity, lest it should be made of no effect!

The early missionaries in Greenland supposed that they must spend a long time in preliminary teaching, preparing the natives to understand the gospel. They taught them the principles of the Old Testament, the law of God, etc., but without spiritual fruit. But one day, when the missionary happened to read the story of the third chapter of John, the old chief was overwhelmed with wonder and joy, and immediately spiritual fruit began, and he and many of his people gladly accepted the Savior of sinners.

One of the most remarkable results that we ever saw follow a single sermon occurred through the preaching of a plain evangelist, especially on one occasion when his discourse was, humanly speaking, weaker than ever before. It lacked animation and rhetorical effect and consisted simply of a clear, plain and rather dry statement of the resurrection of Jesus Christ as the ground of the sinner's hope. But the Holy Spirit used that simple truth to the conversion of a great number of people that night, many of whom remain until this day monuments of the grace of God.

There is in the gospel itself a divine potency that we may fully trust, when we present it in the power of the Spirit, to become God's instrument unto the salvation of all that believe. It has power

to transform the whole eternal destiny of the soul
and to change its entire views of God and motives
of life.

Let us be sure that we do not dilute its power
by trying to mix with it our human reasonings. *or*
Let us be careful that we do not depend unduly
upon the clearness or persuasiveness of our appeal,
but wholly upon the truth of the gospel itself and
the power of the Spirit that accompanies it.

It is a transforming power. While the Spirit is
the worker, He prepares the vessel through which
He works to be a fitting instrument for His service.

Let us look at some of the elements of power
with which the Holy Spirit endues the consecrated heart.

1. Earnestness. This is perhaps the most obvious
quality of a Spirit-filled life. It is that intense fus-
ing of all the capacities of the soul and being into
one's work. It is the secret of success even in human affairs, but it is preeminently the very element of power in Christian workers. It is a quality
which the hearer instinctively discovers and
whose absence is fatal to effectiveness in spite of
all other gifts. Its essential root is sincerity and
honesty of purpose.

It was this which made the Master say, " 'My
food,' said Jesus, 'is to do the will of him who sent
me and to finish his work' " (John 4:34). It was
this which enabled Paul to explain, "If we are out
of our mind, it is for the sake of God. . . . For
Christ's love compels us" (2 Corinthians 5:13-14).

"Brothers, my heart's desire and prayer to God for the Israelites is that they may be saved" (Romans 10:1).

This was the secret of Whitefield's wonderful power; his whole soul was engrossed in his work. His one business was to preach the gospel and win souls. No sacrifice could appall him or deter him from his delightful task. It was an enthusiasm with him, and so it is with every earnest soul. This is the true meaning of the word enthusiasm, which literally signifies, "God within us." Where the Holy Spirit possesses the heart there always is intense enthusiasm. The true minister should be both a burning and shining light, and the baptism of fire is always a baptism of intense earnestness.

2. Holiness. There is a certain atmosphere which a saintly soul carries with him which communicates itself to others and is instinctively perceived even by the careless. There are men and women who awaken in all they come in contact with an irresistible respect, and even reverence. The spirit of godliness, like the nature of the rose, betrays itself in the look, the tone, the bearing, and awakens an unconscious response even in the hearts of ungodly men. The good man compels the homage of the bad, even when he hates and persecutes him.

The very look of the saintly McCheyne often filled the hearts of his hearers with strange solemnity. The tones with which George Whitefield pronounced the simplest word sometimes made people weep. The godless Chesterfield declared, after a visit to Fenelon, that another day in his house would have made him a Christian in spite of himself. The very factory hands were sometimes smitten with conviction at their work as Charles Finney passed through the room. The influence of the Countess of Huntington was such, through her simple piety, that even her profligate king respected her and said he would be glad to go to heaven clinging to her skirts.

It is possible for us, like a spice ship entering the harbor and filling the air with fragrance, to bear about with us the atmosphere of heaven. Then it shall be true of us as it was of the apostles, "For we are to God the aroma of Christ among those who are being saved and those who are perishing. To the one we are the smell of death; to the other, the fragrance of life. And who is equal to such a task?" (2 Corinthians 2:15-16).

The Christian worker, the divine messenger who comes to men fresh from communion with the skies, will have, like Moses, some of the glory upon his brow, and the world will again take knowledge of him that he has been with Jesus. It was said of the good Mr. Aitkin, of England, the father of the well-known evangelist, that one always felt in his presence as though encompassed with the very presence of God. He seemed to carry so much of Christ about with him that people forgot the man in the overshadowing glory of the Master. This is the honor and the power which He will bestow upon every consecrated servant.

3. *Faith.* Our success will bear proportion to our expectation of results. The motto of the effective

worker will be, "We also believe, and therefore speak" (2 Corinthians 4:13, KJV).

A minister complained to Mr. Spurgeon that he thought that he must give up his ministry and doubted if he had ever been called to it, giving as a reason that he had labored untiringly for four years and had not seen a single fruit from his ministry. Mr. Spurgeon simply asked: "Have you always preached expecting conversions at each service?" He acknowledged that he had never thought of such a thing, but had eagerly desired them and wondered why they did not come. "Why," said the good minister, "you did not expect them and you did not receive them; God's condition of blessing is faith; and it is as necessary for our work as for our salvation."

This is indeed true; it is not in proportion to our desperate efforts that we should see the results, but to our simple trust in the power of God to honor His own Word and work by His own Spirit in the hearts of men. Most of the great revival movements have thus begun.

A humble working man in the north of Ireland read the story of George Muller's life and immediately thought, "Why cannot I have the same answer to prayer in the salvation of souls?" He immediately began to pray for a great outpouring of the Holy Spirit upon his city and country. Soon he was joined by another, and then another, and before long a flood of fire was sweeping over all the land, and hundreds of thousands of souls were mightily converted to God. It was thus that Mr. Finney al-

ways prepared for his work. We can read in his bi-
ography how he used to retire with a friend, sometimes into the woods, and spend hours on his knees
until he felt the blessing was claimed and the power
was coming. Then he would go forth about his
work with the tranquil certainty that God was
there and would be revealed in all His power and
glory, and the result always was the mighty working of the Holy Spirit.

Not always is it the preacher who exercises the
effectual faith; sometimes it is a silent and obscure
heart whom no one shall know until the day when
all things shall be revealed.

A celebrated preacher of the Middle Ages was
always accompanied by a quiet and insignificant
man, without whom he would never preach. The
man never opened his lips in public and seemed to
be a useless appendage. The preacher afterward
explained that while he preached his companion
prayed, and he attributed the marvelous results of
his messages to his believing intercessions. There
is no Christian who cannot claim and exercise the
very power of God even in the most silent capacity, and it will be found in the great day that God
has not failed to credit the reward to the real instrument through whom the divine working came.
It will very likely be found in that day that the
voice that spoke from the pulpit had but a frac-
tional share in the real work which the Holy Spirit
accomplished, but that some humble saint was the
real channel through whom the fire of God fell
upon convicted and converted souls.

But it is not only for the conversion of souls that God will give us His power and faith to claim His working, but for everything connected with His cause, and our ministry shall touch every part of His work.

Faith is the true channel of effectiveness, simply because faith is merely the hand by which the forces of Omnipotence are brought to bear upon the work. The removing of obstacles, the influencing of human hearts and minds, the bringing together of workers, the obtaining of helpers, the supply of financial needs—all these are proper subjects for believing prayer and proper lines for demonstrating the all-sufficiency of God. And if, instead of begging for help and compromising the honor of Christ by despairing appeals to the church and the world, the people of God would more simply trust Him, they would be saved a thousand embarrassments. Then His name would be constantly glorified in the manifestation of His all-sufficiency before an unbelieving world.

A few stupendous examples of God's faithfulness in answering the prayers of His people in the supply of money and men, such as have been afforded by the story of George Muller's orphanage, the China Inland Mission and similar works of faith, were not intended to be isolated instances, but to prove to the world that Christ is able always to meet His people's needs. These are but samples of a principle which should be the rule of Christian work—that God in all things might be glorified through Jesus Christ, not only in the spiritual, but in the temporal and practical needs of His kingdom.

4. Love. Still more necessary is the spirit of love as the very element and character of every true Christian worker. "[D]o you truly love me?" (John 21:16) is the prime condition on which Christ's saints are to minister to His flock. Love for souls is the only bond that can win and hold them and can sustain our own heart amid the trials and discouragements of Christian work. Human love will make any task a delight. For the child she loves the mother can toil and suffer without weariness, and count life itself a small sacrifice.

We must love people if we would do them good, but such love must be divine. Mere human sympathy does not go to the depths of their heart, but the love which is born of God and inbreathed of the Holy Spirit finds its way to the very citadel of rebellion and wins the soul for God.

There is much danger of turning the gospel of Christ and the power of God into human sentiment. Mere compassion for people, and even a costly show of interest and sympathy, will not save them, but the love born of the Holy Spirit will go as deep as the height from which it springs. If we walk in the Spirit He will breathe upon us that love which will brood over souls, loving them even before we know them, praying for them in the Spirit before we have singled them out. Then when we meet them we will recognize them with a thrill of joy as the souls that we have been bearing on our hearts as a burden of prayer.

This love will strangely endear to us even the unlovely and make the most dreadful scenes more delightful than the surroundings of culture and affection and a life of luxury and indulgence. This is the passion that has drawn so many outstanding men and women to the wretched fields of sin until their heavenly love has gathered, like the magnet to itself, the lost and wretched, and bound them forever to the heart of Christ. This is the best and highest gift of the Holy Spirit: the most tender, irresistible element of spiritual power.

This was the force that drew souls to Jesus, who loved them to Himself. He was the Shepherd on the mountains, facing every privation and peril to find the sheep that was lost. He was the weary wayfarer by Samaria's well, longing for the heart of that poor woman more than for meat and drink. He was the tender face that looked on Peter and broke his heart by a single glance of love. He is the voice that still says to each rescued, ransomed soul, "I have loved you with an everlasting love; I have drawn you with loving-kindness" (Jeremiah 31:3).

This was the power of Paul's ministry. How he loved his flock! "[W]e were delighted to share with you . . . our lives" (1 Thessalonians 2:8); "[W]e dealt with each of you as a father deals with his own children (1 Thessalonians 2:11); "[W]e were gentle among you, like a mother caring for her little children" (1 Thessalonians 2:7); "I could wish that I myself were cursed and cut off from

Christ for the sake of my brothers, those of my own race" (Romans 9:3). Men can make burning glasses of iron which will confront the solar rays and kindle fires in polar seas. Not so can souls be set on fire; the medium must itself be glowing and burning, "a lamp that burned and gave light" (John 5:35).

5) Tact. This is difficult to describe. It expresses a kind of heavenly wisdom, a holy judiciousness and fitness of manner and method which adapts itself by the teaching of the Spirit to diversities of character, and in a proper sense becomes all things to all men that it may win some. "[H]e who wins souls," the preacher says, "is wise" (Proverbs 11:30). "I will make you fishers of men" (Matthew 4:19), said the Master. "I caught you by trickery" (2 Corinthians 12:16), says the apostle Paul.

The word tact literally means "touch." There are many kinds of touch. There is the touch of a mother which even the dying boy can recognize when unconscious of all else, and there is the touch of a blacksmith or a policeman. Not thus are we to touch the souls with which we are dealing for eternity. He that possesses the Holy Spirit will have a holy deference that will feel its way to their hearts, gently approaching them, dispelling their prejudices, being tolerant of their faults, patient with their dullness or slowness and pressing steadily and wisely to the goal of their hearts.

So the Lord drew to Him the woman at Jacob's well. First, He awakened her interest; second, He disarmed her prejudices and won her confidence.

Next, He awakened the hunger in her heart. Then
He ventured to arouse her conscience to the recol-
lection of its sin, carefully avoiding any contro-
versy about doctrines and religions, until at last
He bore straight to her heart the revelation of
Himself as her Savior.

Nothing can teach tact but the Holy Spirit and a
heart so full of love for souls that it is vigilant from
its very desire to win them. It is the very wisdom of
the Holy Spirit and of the heart of love. There is
only One that can make us fishers of men. This
power is not always manifest in the public discourse or the wholesale dealing with souls. He
Himself charges every minister to reap, even as
reapers gather their sheaves by hand one by one.
And he who is not willing thus to seek and find the
lost by personal, patient, wise and loving ministry
shall never know the fullness of the Spirit of power.

We have to learn that no two hearts can be dealt
with on general principles and in the same way.
The message that was blessed yesterday to a special assembly may not be the one for today. The
promise, the incident, the illustration which
helped that one to the Savior cannot be applied as
a cast-iron pattern to the next one. In each case we
must be distinctly led by the Spirit of wisdom and
grace, and if we trust Him, "[a]t that time you will
be given what to say" (Matthew 10:19).

Thanks be to His name who has promised us
something better than our poor, weak common
sense, even that divine enduement, the Spirit of
power and of love, and of a sound mind.

The Conditions of Spiritual Power

Of course, the prime condition is that we ourselves are walking in holiness and obedience and pleasing the Holy Spirit for our own life. We cannot expect to impart to others what we do not possess ourselves. There is nothing that tells on human souls like reality, and men instinctively know whether we have experienced what we teach.

No man has a right to give to others what he has not tasted and tested himself. The mightiest force in all our work is to know and to have all men know that our life is back of our work.

The next condition is that we work on scriptural lines. We cannot expect the power of God to accompany a minister or a church, to any great extent, which allows itself to be compromised by entanglements with the world or with methods which are contrary to Scripture. We cannot expect a lasting revival to follow a series of religious entertainments or to be followed by a scene of dissipation or spiritual relaxation. The church and minister who may expect the most divine and abiding fruit are they who always work on strictly spiritual lines, and in simple accordance with the Word of God.

We must be careful of resorting too much to human attractions to draw people to Christ. There is a sense in which it is quite proper to use the legitimate power of consecrated music and the social element to promote a congenial and radiant spirit in the work and worship of God. But a work which has to be sustained by the aid of social receptions, musical entertainments and the operatic stage behind the pulpit, can never be sanctioned or crowned by the power of the Holy Spirit to any considerable extent.

In spite of these things, God does make the best He can of His own truth and the baffled efforts of His individual people even in such a work. It is a sad, hopeless confusion, however, and always leads to ultimate disappointment and impermanent results.

In order to enjoy the power of God we must use His own instrumentalities and weapons—His Holy Word and a simple, pure and full gospel. These are the weapons of our warfare, which are not carnal but mighty through God to the pulling down of strongholds; and if we would expect His power we must preach His truth in faithfulness and fullness. And it shall prevail, if proclaimed in the spirit of faith and love.

Many sermons do not possess enough of truth to give them converting power. The Holy Spirit cannot use fully a mere appeal to the sensibilities or even to the fears of an audience. An inspired messenger should present Christ and Him crucified, and where this is done the Holy Spirit will make it the power of God unto salvation, if His working is rightly claimed and expected.

Finally, our motive must be pure in seeking the glory of Christ. Merely to desire power that we may be powerful preachers or successful workers will bring bitter disappointment. God will not lend the Holy Spirit to any man to dishonor His own dear Son. He shall testify of Jesus, and not to any man. Self must be dead, and Christ alone exalted, if we are to have much of the power of God.

Some men cannot stand much usefulness, and God loves them too much to set them on the pinnacle of a temple, for there is no fall so great as that which falls from great heights. There is no sacrilege so dangerous and shameful as that which uses the gifts of God to glorify any man. Not only must every faithful minister fear for himself the faintest shadow of self-consciousness, but his people must ever guard him from the peril of their own idolatry. As surely as they recognize in him anything but God, they do him cruel harm, and bring upon him humiliation and loss.

An old fisherman was asked how he was so successful. He gave the very sensible answer that he always kept himself out of sight of the fish; and many a minister and worker may find a hint of their failure in this simple illustration.

When Alexander the Great first met his famous warhorse, Bucephalous, he found that the animal became terrified whenever he turned his back to the sun, because his own shadow was thrown before him and, like a specter, haunted his vision and hindered his progress. The wise hero instantly leaped into the saddle, turned his face to the sun, threw his shadow behind, plunged his spurs into his steed and galloped off in majestic style to the amazement of his beholders. From that hour the steed was his master's inseparable companion and led many an invincible charge—and always to victory.

So let us throw our shadow behind us, set our faces toward Christ and press on in the power of God to victorious service and at last to imperishable glory.

The Spirit of Prayer

In the same way, the Spirit helps us in our weakness. We do not know what we ought to pray for, but the Spirit himself intercedes for us with groans that words cannot express. (Romans 8:26)

The mystery of prayer! There is nothing like it in the natural universe. A higher and a lower being in perfect communion. A familiar intercourse, yet both as widely distinct as the finite is from the infinite. More wonderful even than that we should be able to hold converse with the insect that crawls beneath our feet or the bird that flutters on the branches at our window! Marvelous bond of prayer which can span the gulf between the Creator and the creature, the infinite God and the humblest and most illiterate child!

How has this been accomplished? The three divine Persons have all cooperated in opening the es of prayer. The Father waits at the throne of grace as the hearer of prayer; the Son has come to reveal the Father and has returned to be our Advocate in His presence. And the Holy Spirit has come still nearer, as the other Advocate in the hearts, to teach us the heavenly secret of prayer and send up our petitions in the true spirit to the hands of our heavenly Intercessor. It is this ministry we consider now.

The very name given to the Holy Spirit literally means "the Advocate," and the chief business of the one Advocate is to prepare our cause in the office and to plead it before the Judge. We have the whole Trinity in our behalf. The Holy Spirit prepares our case, the Lord Jesus presents it and the Judge is our Father. What an infinite light, and what an unspeakable comfort this sheds on the subject of prayer!

Our need of this Advocate is referred to very impressively in Romans 8:26—"We do not know what we ought to pray for." We are often ignorant of the subjects for which we ought to pray. Often, when we know our needs, we know not how rightly to present them. There is much expressed in these words. We are often deeply ignorant of our truest needs, and the things we wish most for are not the things we most require. Our minds are blinded by prejudice and passion; the things we would sometimes ask for we shall afterwards find would have been only an injury. Besides, we know not the future and cannot intelligently anticipate the needs and dangers against which we should pray, while a thousand unseen elements of peril continually surround us and need a wiser forethought and insight than our own to guard against.

The right motive which seeks supremely the glory of God; the right spirit recognizing submissively and joyfully His sovereign will; the deep and sincere desire; the faith which dares to ask as largely as the measure of the Father's will and promise; the patience that tarries if it waits, knowing that it will surely come and will not tarry too long; the obedience that steps out upon the promise—all these elements of prayer are operations of the Holy Spirit, and we cannot too devoutly thank Him that He is willing thus to teach our ignorance and simplicity the heavenly secret of prayer. "[T]he Spirit helps us in our weakness. . . . [T]he Spirit himself intercedes for us with groans that words cannot express" (Romans 8:26).

The Holy Spirit reveals to us our needs. This is always the first element in prayer, a painful consciousness of failure and necessity. The prophet's word to Jehoshaphat was, "Make this valley full of ditches" (2 Kings 3:16), and then the second, "[T]his valley will be filled with water" (3:17). The heart must be plowed up into great channels of conscious need to hold the blessing when it comes. This is often painful work, but "[b]lessed are those who hunger and thirst for righteousness, for they will be filled" (Matthew 5:6).

When the Spirit of grace and supplication is poured out upon Jerusalem, the effect is a deep

and universal sorrow. "They will look on me, the
one they have pierced, and they will mourn for
him as one mourns for an only child, and grieve
bitterly for him as one grieves for a firstborn son"
(Zechariah 12:10). The Spirit of prayer is the
spirit of dependence, deep humility and conscious
need.

The Holy Spirit next awakens in the soul holy
desires for the blessings that God is about to give.
Desire is an element in prayer. "[W]hatever you
ask for in prayer," our Lord says, "believe that you
have received it" (Mark 11:24). These deep spiritual longings are like the rootlets by which the
plant draws the nourishment from the soil, like
the absorbing vessels of the human system which
take in and assimilate nourishment and food. The
desires give intensity and force to our prayer and
enlarge the heart to receive the blessing when it
comes. God, therefore, often keeps His children
waiting for the visible answer to their petitions in
order that they may more ardently desire the
blessing and be thus enabled to receive it more
fully and appreciate it more when it comes.

When we were traveling in Italy, we were
often serenaded by parties of native musicians
whose sweet strains were sometimes very delightful. But we noticed that whenever we paid
them their little gratuity they always stopped
the music and went away. When we wished to
listen longer to their playing, we waited before
paying them. So God loves to hear His people's
holy desires and earnest prayers and often pro-

longs the petition because He delights to hear us pray, and then gives us the larger blessing in proportion to our waiting. Has your heart ever longed for some special blessing until it seemed that it would break for desire? You almost thought that you never would possess the holiness for which you longed. But now as you look back you see that this deep hunger was just the beginning of your blessing. It was the shadow side, the Holy Spirit awakening all the receptive capacities of your being to absorb it when it came.

Once we saw a party of children sending up a balloon of tissue paper. First, the balloon was carefully constructed of the lightest fabric and then suspended with light cords a few feet above the ground. A small light was attached, and then they began to prepare the force that was to be used for its ascension. It involved nothing more than simply building a little fire below the open mouth of the balloon and allowing the heated air to ascend until it filled the entire space within. The moment this was done the little vessel swelled and reached out for its ascension, pulling hard at the restraining cords and pressing upwards. When it was thoroughly filled with the heated air, it was only necessary to cut the cords and instantly it sailed away into the upper air.

So it seems the warm breath of holy desire and earnest purpose in prayer, when inspired by the Holy Spirit, bears up our petitions to the throne of grace and makes the difference between the mere words of formalism and the "prayer of a righteous man [that] is powerful and effective" (James 5:16).

The Holy Spirit lays upon the heart in which He dwells the special burden of prayer. We often read in the old prophetic Scriptures of the burden of the Lord. Even now the Lord lays His burden on His consecrated messengers. This is the meaning of the strong language of our text, "[T]he Spirit himself intercedes for us with groans that words cannot express" (Romans 8:26).

Sometimes this burden is inarticulate and unintelligible even to the suppliant himself. Perhaps some heavy shadow rests upon the soul, some deep depression, some crushing weight under which we can only groan. With it there may come the definite thought of some personal need, some apprehended evil that overhangs us or some dear one who is brought to our spirit as somehow connected with the pressure. As we pray for this special person or thing, light seems to open upon the heart and an assurance of having met the will of God in our prayer. Or sometimes the burden is not understood; and yet, as it presses heavily upon us and we hold it up to Him who does understand, we are conscious that our prayer is not in vain. He who knows its meaning and prompts its cry is granting what He sees to be best under the circumstances for us or others, as the burden may apply.

We may never know in this world just what it meant, and yet often we shall find that some great trial has been averted, some impending danger turned aside, some difficulty overcome, some sufferer relieved, some soul saved.

It is not necessary that we should always know. Indeed, perhaps we should never fully know what any of our prayers wholly mean. God's answer is always larger than our petition, and even when our prayer is most definite and intelligent there is a wide margin which only the Holy Spirit can interpret, and God will fill it up in His infinite wisdom and love. That is what is meant by the significant language of the text, "And he who searches our hearts knows the mind of the Spirit, because the Spirit intercedes for the saints in accordance with God's will" (Romans 8:27).

The Father is always searching our hearts and listening, not to our wild and often mistaken outcries, but to the mind of the Holy Spirit in us, whom He recognizes as our true Guardian and Monitor, and He grants us according to His petitions and not merely our words. But if we walk in the Spirit and are trained to know and obey His voice, we shall not send up the wild and vain outcries of our mistaken impulses, but shall echo His will and His prayer and shall always pray in accordance with the will of God.

The sensitive spirit learns very quickly to discern God's voice. That which would naturally be considered as simple depression of spirits comes to be instantly recognized as a hint that God has something to say to us or something to ask in us for ourselves or others. Often our physical sensations come to be quick, instinctive interpreters of some inward call, for when we do not quickly listen to God's voice He knocks more loudly until the very body feels the pain and warns us that the Lord has need of us. If we were more watchful we would find that nothing comes to us at any moment of our lives which has not some divine significance, which does not lead us in some way to communion or service. He who thus walks with God soon learns the luxury of having no personal burdens or troubles, but recognizes everything as service for God or for others.

This makes the ministry of prayer a very solemn responsibility. For if we are not obedient to His voice, some interest must suffer, some part of His will be neglected, some part of His purpose frustrated—so far, at least, as our cooperation is concerned. And perhaps someone very dear to us will lose a blessing through our neglect or disobedience. We ourselves may find that we are not prepared for the conflict or trial against which He was providing by the very burden that we would not understand or carry.

Thus it was with the disciples and the Master in the garden of Gethsemane. That was for Him the anticipation of the cross. As He met the burden in advance, He was prepared for the awful hours that followed, went through them in victory and thus redeemed the world. But the disciples could not watch with Him one hour. They neglected the call to prayer and slept when they should have been attentive and praying. The result was that the morning found them unprepared, and the trial ended in

shameful failure. Only the Master's previous intercession for him saved Peter from entire wreck and
perhaps a fate as desperate as that of Judas.

God has placed within our breast a Monitor
who is always looking forward to our needs and
anticipating our situations. Let us, therefore, be
quick to obey His voice as He calls us to the ministry of prayer, and in so doing we shall not only
save ourselves but also others who perhaps are not
able to pray for themselves.

The Spirit brings to our hearts, in the ministry
of prayer, the encouragement of God's Word, the
promises of His grace and the fullness of Christ to
meet our need. It is He who gives us such conceptions of Christ as awaken in us confidence of
blessing. He opens to our vision the infinite resources of the grace of God and shows us all the
rich provision of our Father's house. He unfolds to
us the grounds of faith in the gospel and teaches
us to understand our redemption rights, our filial
claims and our high calling in Christ Jesus. He
breathes in our heart the Spirit of sonship, and He
inspires the faith which is the essential condition
of effectual prayer. And so He leads us to present
to the Father, in the name of the Lord Jesus, not
only the right desires but in the right spirit: "For
through him we both have access to the Father by
one Spirit" (Ephesians 2:18).

Thus He is in us the Spirit of faith, the Spirit of
adoption, the Spirit of liberty in prayer, the Spirit
of holy confidence and enlargement of heart, and
the witnessing Spirit—who, when we pray in

faith, seals upon our soul the divine assurance that our prayer is accepted before God and that the answer will be surely given. We must first, however, believe God's promise in the exercise of simple faith. As we do, the Spirit witnesses with our spirit and often fills the soul with joy and praise which anticipates the answer long before it is apparent. This is the highest triumph of prayer—to look within the veil, even before the curtains are parted, and know that our petition is granted; to hear the sound of the bells upon our High Priest's garment, even from the inmost chambers; and to rejoice in the anticipation of our blessing as fully as if we already saw its complete fulfillment.

Our Lord always requires this faith as the condition of answered prayer. "Therefore, I tell you, whatever you ask for in prayer, believe that you have received it, and it will be yours" (Mark 11:24). "But when he asks, he must believe and not doubt, because he who doubts is like a wave of the sea, blown and tossed by the wind. That man should not think he will receive anything from the Lord" (James 1:6-7).

But this is the special work of the Holy Spirit. He is the Spirit of revelation and of faith, and as we pray in His fellowship and according to His will, we shall be enabled through His grace to ask with humble and confident expectation of His blessing.

The Holy Spirit will also teach us when to cease from prayer and turn our petition into thanksgiving. He may bid us go out in obedience

to meet the answer as it waits before us or comes
to meet us. There is a place for silence as well as
prayer. When we truly believe, we shall cease to
ask as we asked before, and then our prayers shall
simply be in the attitude of waiting for our answer, or holding up God's promise to Him in the
Spirit of praise and expectation.

This does not mean that we shall never think
anymore about that for which we asked, but we
shall not think of it in a doubtful manner. We shall
think of it only with thanksgiving and restful expectation. We may often remind God of it, but it
will always be in the spirit of trust and confidence.
Therefore, the prophet speaks of those who are
"the Lord's remembrancers," those who remind
God of His promises and wait upon Him for His
fulfillment of them. This is really a spirit of
prayer, and yet it is not perhaps a spirit of petition
so much as praise, which indeed is the true exhibi-
tion of the highest form of faith.

Sometimes, too, after our prayer the Holy
Spirit will have a subsequent ministry of obedience for us. Perhaps there will be something for us
to do in receiving the answer, and He will show
us, interpreting to us God's providences as they
meet us and enabling us to meet them in a spirit of
cooperation and vigilance.

He also will be present to support our faith in
its tests and painful trials and to enable us to rejoice and praise God, often in the seeming contra-
dictions of His providence. For faith is always
tested, and "[y]ou need to persevere so that when

you have done the will of God, you will receive
what he has promised" (Hebrews 10:36).

Cooperating with the Holy Spirit

Receive the Holy Spirit. (John 20:22)
[B]e filled with the Spirit. (Ephesians 5:18)

While we recognize the sovereign power of the Holy Spirit, visiting the heart at His pleasure and working according to His will upon the objects of His grace, yet God has ordained certain laws of operation and cooperation in connection with the application of redemption. And He Himself most delicately recognizes His own laws and respects the freedom of the human will. He does not force His blessings upon unwilling hearts, but knocks at the door of our hearts, waiting to be recognized and claimed, and then working in the soul as we heartily cooperate, hear and obey. There is, therefore, a very solemn and responsible part for every man in cooperating with the Holy Spirit.

"Now to each one the manifestation of the Spirit is given for the common good" (1 Corinthians 12:7)—that is to say, it rests with the man who receives the first movement of the Holy Spirit to determine how far he will embrace his opportunity, cooperate with his heavenly Friend and enter into all the fullness of the good and perfect will of God.

Perhaps the talent, represented in the parable as given to every one of the servants, was meant to express that gift of the Spirit which every Christian receives, and the various uses which the servants made of this common enduement may represent the degrees with which the children of God use their spiritual advantages.

One improved his talent until it had become 10; another until it had increased fivefold; another neglected it and hid it in the earth. So three men receiving in the beginning of their experience an equal measure of spiritual things may show in the end just as great a diversity in the use that they have made of the precious trust. By a diligent and vigilant obedience the one has grown to be a Paul, crowned with ransomed souls and clothed with all the fullness of heavenly power. The other has become, perhaps, a proud Diotrephes, seeking chiefly his personal ambition and using the divine grace for his own advantage.

The Holy Spirit is especially sensitive to the reception He finds in the human heart, never intruding as an unwelcome Guest but gladly entering every open door and following up every invitation with His faithful love and power. How are we to cooperate with Him?

Let Us Receive the Holy Spirit

This denotes an active and positive taking of His life and power into our hearts and lives. It is not a mere acquiescence in His coming or passive assent to His will, but an active appropriating and absorbing of His blessed person and influences into our whole being. It is one thing to have our dinner brought to us, and it is another thing to eat it, drink it, assimilate it and be nourished by it.

We are to receive the Holy Spirit with an open, yielding, hungering, thirsting, believing, accepting and absorbing heart, even as the dry sand receives the rain, as the empty sponge receives the moisture, as the negative cloud receives the current from the positive, as the vacuum receives the air and the baby drinks in the mother's life from her offered breast.

There are spiritual organs of reception as well as physical. There are vessels of heart-hunger and absorption which can be cultivated and exercised, and there are those "who by reason of use have their senses exercised to discern both good and evil" (Hebrews 5:14, KJV) to receive the grace of God.

Are we receiving the Holy Spirit? Are we taking the water of life freely? Are we putting forth our hand and grasping the tree of life and eating of its fruit?

Let us remember that we are receiving a Person, and that in order to do so we must recognize that Person individually and treat Him as we would a welcome guest.

Have we received the Holy Spirit as a Person, invited Him into our hearts, believed that He really came and then begun to treat Him as an actual person? Do we talk to Him, commune with Him, enjoy His fellowship, call upon His help and practically recognize Him as a present Guest?

Not only do we receive the Holy Spirit as a Person, but having thus recognized Him we are to receive His influences as He imparts them, to be open to His touch, attentive to His voice, responsive to His love, and to be empty vessels for His constant use and filling.

Let Us Be Filled with the Spirit

While it is true that there is a definite moment when the Holy Spirit comes to reside in the heart, yet there are repeated experiences of His renewing, quickening, reviving, refreshing influences. These are called by the apostle Paul the "renewal by the Holy Spirit" (Titus 3:5), which He sheds on us abundantly, and by Peter, in the Acts of the Apostles, "that times of refreshing may come from the Lord" (3:19). The expression "baptized with the Holy Spirit" (1:5), may be applied perhaps to our first marked experience of this kind. In this connection we are glad that the term baptism means a very thorough and complete immersion in the ocean of His love and fullness.

But it is not once that He is asked to manifest His love and power. We read in the Acts of the Apostles that after the day of Pentecost there came another day when the disciples were assembled in a time of peril and trial in prayer before the Master for His interposition. When they had prayed, the place was shaken where they had assembled, and they were all filled with the Holy Spirit, and the mighty power of God was manifested afresh in their midst.

And so Paul says in Ephesians, "Do not get drunk on wine. . . . Instead, be filled with the Spirit" (Ephesians 5:18). The filling of the Spirit is here contrasted with the exciting influence of earthly stimulants, as if he had said, "There is one draught of which you can never drink too much; you can safely be intoxicated with the Holy Spirit."

Paul uses the same expression in connection with the figure of baptism: "For we were all baptized by one Spirit into one body . . . and we were all given the one Spirit to drink" (1 Corinthians 12:13). It is the figure of being submerged in the ocean and then, when lost in the depths of the sea, opening our mouths and beginning to drink of its depths and fullness. We are plunged into the Holy Spirit until He becomes the element of our being, like the air in which we move, and then we open all the faculties of our being and drink from His inexhaustible supplies.

How great the capacity of the human soul to be filled with the life of God it is impossible to say.

Surely, if the sun can fill a flower with its glorious light in all the many-tinted colors; surely, if the cloud can drink in its rays until it glows with all the tints of light, then surely the human soul can absorb all there is in God and then give it forth in the reflected light of holiness. Surely, if the earth can drink in the rain and then give it out in the plants and fruits and flowers of summer, the human heart can draw from God the elements of His very being and turn them into all the fruits of holy living and useful deeds. Surely, if His own beloved Son could dwell in His bosom ages upon ages before an angel ever sang or a planet swept along its heavenly way or an object of creation filled the plains of immensity, and could find in His Father's heart the rapture of His joy so that He could say, "I was filled with delight day after day, rejoicing always in his presence" (Proverbs 8:30)—then surely the human soul can fill all its little vessels and satisfy the measure of its capacities in His divine love and kindness.

Let us receive Him in all His fullness; let us be filled with the Spirit; let us drink of the ocean in which we have been baptized. A Christian friend wrote that his old neighbors were circulating a report that he had turned out badly in his Christian life and taken to drinking. He replied, very happily, that it was true he had been drinking of late, but that if his old friends could only know what he was drinking they would all join him. For he had found the fountain of living waters and was drinking from the Holy Spirit and, as Jesus said,

"[W]hoever drinks the water I give him will never thirst" (John 4:14).

Let Us Trust the Holy Spirit

We must believe in the Spirit as well as in the Son and treat Him with confidence, expecting Him to meet us and bless us as we communicate unto Him all our needs, perplexities and even our temptations and sins. He is the anti-type of the water of Horeb's ancient rock. It is as wrong today as it was for Moses to strike that rock in unbelieving violence when God bids us simply to speak to it in gentleness and trust and to expect its waters to gush forth at our whispered call and satisfy our every need.

The Holy Spirit is sensitive to our distrust. Many persons cry for Him and pray to Him as though He were a distant and selfish tyrant, insensible to His children's cry. It is a mother's heart to whom we speak and one who is always within whispering distance of her little ones.

Let us nestle beneath her wings; let us walk in the light of her love; let us trust the Holy Spirit with implicit, childlike confidence and always expect the answering voice and presence of the Comforter. Then it shall be true: "Before they call I will answer; while they are still speaking I will hear" (Isaiah 65:24). The apostle Paul asks the Galatians, "Did you receive the Spirit by observing the law, or by believing what you heard?" (Galatians 3:2), and adds after, "so that by faith we might receive the promise of the Spirit" (3:14).

This is the only way that we can receive a person—by treating him with confidence, believing that he comes to us in sincerity and, opening the door to him at once, recognize him as a friend and treat him as a welcome guest. So let us treat the Holy Spirit.

Let Us Obey the Spirit

The first thing in obedience is to listen. Especially is this necessary with the gentle Comforter. So gentle is this Mother that her voice is not often loud and may be missed by the inattentive ear. Therefore the beautiful expression is used by the apostle Paul in the eighth chapter of Romans, which reminds us of a mother's voice: "but the mind controlled by the Spirit is life and peace" (8:6). We are to obey the Spirit; we are to pay attention to His counsels, commands and slightest intimations. God never speaks an idle word or gives a lesson that we can afford to slight or forget. They who will listen will have much to listen to, but they who slight the voice of God need not wonder that they are often left in silence.

The Spirit's voice is a "still small voice" (1 Kings 19:12, KJV). The heart in which He loves to dwell is a quiet one, where the voice of passion and the world's loud tumult is stilled, and His whisper is watched for with delight and attention.

But not only must we listen; when we know, we must obey. The voice of the Spirit is imperative; there can be no compromise, and there should be no delay. God will not excuse us from

His commandments. His word is very deliberately spoken and for our good always, and when the command is given it cannot be recalled. Therefore if we do not obey we must be involved in darkness, difficulty and separation from Him. We may plunge on, but the Spirit waits at that point on the crossroads of life, and we can make no progress until we return and obey Him.

Many a bitter experience, many a tear of brokenhearted disappointment and failure have come from refusing to obey. Indeed, such disobedience must be fatal if persisted in. It was just there that Saul halted and lost his kingdom through disobedience and willfulness in neglecting the voice of God. It was there that Israel found the fatal crisis of her history at Kadesh-barnea. It was there that, in the apostolic days, a nation was about to reap the same fatal error, and the apostle pleaded with his countrymen so solemnly and gently: "Today, if you hear his voice, do not harden your hearts" (Psalm 95:7-8).

Happy the heart that promptly obeys the voice of God. The Spirit delights to lead such a soul. How beautifully we see this illustrated in the experience of Paul! At one period of his ministry he was in danger of pressing on in his work beyond the divine command, and so, we are told, he was forbidden of the Spirit to preach the Word in Asia, and "tried to enter Bithynia, but the Spirit of Jesus would not allow them to" (Acts 16:7). Happy for him that he obeyed both these restraints. Had he persisted in his way and even succeeded in getting down to Ephesus, he would have found every door closed and his visit would have been premature. Waiting on God's bidding and way a year longer, he was permitted to go and found the door wide open, and his next and perhaps most successful ministry was given to him at Ephesus. And in obedience that led him now into Europe, he was permitted to establish the gospel in that mighty continent.

A little later, we see the very opposite lesson exemplified in his life. We are told that he purposed in Spirit to go to Jerusalem and Rome. This was a personal direction of the Holy Spirit to him, and in consequence he determined upon the greatest purpose of his life—to carry the gospel to his countrymen at Jerusalem and then to establish Christianity in the capitals of the world.

It was well that he proposed it in the Spirit and that he was sure of God's command, for the difficulties that afterward met him would have seemed insurmountable.

First, the very servants of God met him all along the way, and even prophetic messengers warned him not to go to Jerusalem, but the brave apostle kept to his promise and pressed on.

Next, the whole power of unbelieving Judaism arrayed itself against him, tried to mob him at Jerusalem, to assassinate him on the way to Caesarea and then to condemn him before the tribunal of Felix, Festus and Agrippa. Still he pressed steadfastly on.

Next, the intriguing policy and imperial power

of Rome itself confronted him and held him two years a prisoner at Caesarea, but he never for a moment abandoned his purpose.

At length he was on his way to Rome, but then the very elements of nature and the powers of hell combined in one last effort to destroy him. The fierce Euroclydon of the Mediterranean wrecked his ship, and on Malta's shore a viper from the flames fastened upon his hand, but he still pressed on in indomitable might in obedience to the Holy Spirit. And so he reached Rome and planted the standard of the cross before the palace of the Caesars, witnessed for Christ in the face of imprisonment and martyrdom and at last looked down from heaven on the spectacle of Christianity as the established religion of the whole Roman empire 300 years later.

Let us obey the Holy Spirit, whether it be in silence or in activity, and we shall find that if He be to us our Wonderful Counselor, He shall certainly prove our Mighty God.

Let Us Honor the Holy Spirit

Less than any other person does He honor Himself. His constant business is to exalt Christ and hide behind His person. Therefore, the Father is pleased when we exalt and honor Him, and He himself will especially use the instrument which gives Him the glory. "Honor the Holy Spirit and He will honor you," was the counsel of an aged Christian patriarch who had seen many a

mighty awakening in the church of God. It is indeed true and specially important in this material-
istic and rationalistic age, when even the ministers
of Christ sometimes seem to wish to eliminate the
supernatural from the Scriptures and the church
and find any other explanation than the power of
God for His supernatural working.

The special dispensation of the Holy Spirit is
drawing to its close. We may therefore expect that
He will manifest His power in unusual methods
and degrees as the end of the age draws near.

Let us understand Him and be in sympathy with
His divine thought and ready to follow His wise
and mighty leadership unto the last campaign of
Christianity. Why should we ever be looking back
to Pentecost? Why should we not expect His
mightiest triumphs in the immediate future and, as
Joel had prophesied, "before the coming of the
great and dreadful day of the LORD" (Joel 2:31)?

Hindering the Holy Spirit

*Do not put out the Spirit's fire. (1 Thessalonians
5:19)*
*And do not grieve the Holy Spirit of God. (Ephe-
sians 4:30)*
You always resist the Holy Spirit. (Acts 7:51)

I t is very touching and solemn that while the
Holy Spirit might, in the exercise of His omnipotence, coerce our will and compel us to sub-
mit to His authority, yet He approaches us with
the most deferential regard for our feelings and in-
dependence, even suffering us to resist and disobey Him, and bearing long with our willfulness
and waywardness.

There are several terms used in the Scriptures
to denote the manner in which we may sin against
the Holy Spirit.

We May Quench the Spirit

This has reference, perhaps, mainly to the hindrance we offer to His work in others, rather than to our resistance of His personal dealings with our own souls.

Among the various hindrances which we may offer to the Holy Spirit may be mentioned such as these:

We may refuse to obey His impulses in us when He bids us speak or act for Him. We may be conscious of a distinct impression of the Spirit of God bidding us to testify for Christ, and by disobedience or timidity or procrastination, we may quench His working, both in our own soul and in the heart of another.

We may suppress His voice in others, either by using our authority to restrain His messages when He speaks through His servants or refusing to allow the liberty of testimony. Many hold the reins of ecclesiastical authority unduly, and thus lose the free and effectual working of the Holy Spirit in their churches and in their work.

There is a less direct way, however, of politely silencing Him by forcing Him out, and so filling the atmosphere with the spirit of stiffness, criticism and a certain air of respectability and rigidness that He gently withdraws from the uncongenial scene and refuses to thrust His messages upon unwilling hearts.

The Spirit may be quenched by the method of public worship in a congregation. It may be either so stiff

and formal that there is no room for His spontane-
ous working, or so full of worldly and unscriptural
elements as to repel and offend Him from taking
any part in a pompous ritual. An operatic choir
and a ritualistic service will effectually quench all
the fire of God's altar and cause the gentle Dove
to seek a simpler nest.

4) *The Spirit may be quenched by the preacher, and his
spirit and method.* His own manner may be so intellectual and self-conscious, and his own spirit so
thoroughly cold and vain, that the Holy Spirit is
neither recognized nor known in his work.

His sermons may be on themes in which the
Spirit has no interest, for He only witnesses to the
Holy Scriptures and the Person of Christ. He will
wearily turn away from the discussion of philosophy and the stale show of critical brilliancy over
the questions of the day or the speculations of
man's own vain reason.

Perhaps his address is so rigidly written down
that the Holy Spirit could not find an opportunity
for even a suggestion if He so desired, or His
promptings and leadings are coolly set aside by a
course of elaborate preparation which leaves no
room for God.

The spirit of error in the teachings of the pulpit
will always quench the Holy Spirit. He is jealous
for His own inspired Word, and when vain man
attempts to set it aside He looks on with indigna-
tion and exposes such teachers to humiliation and
failure.

The spirit of self-assertion and self-consciousness is always fatal to the free working of the Holy Spirit. When a man stands up in the sacred desk to air his eloquence and call attention to his intellectual brilliancy, or to preach himself in any sense, he will always be deserted by the Holy Spirit. He uses "the lowly things of this world and the despised things—and the things that are not—to nullify the things that are" (1 Corinthians 1:28). And before we can expect to become the instruments of His power, we must wholly cease from self and be lost in the person and glory of Jesus.

5) *The spirit of pride, fashion and worldly display in the pews is just as fatal as ambition in the pulpit.* Such an atmosphere seems to freeze out the spirit of devotion and erect on the throne of the lowly Nazarene a goddess of carnal pride and pleasure, like the foul Venus that the Parisian mob set up in the Madeleine at Paris in the days of the revolution as an object of worship. From such an atmosphere the Holy Spirit turns away grieved and disgusted.

6) *The quickening and reviving influences of the Holy Spirit are often quenched in the very hour of promise by wrong methods in the work of Christ's church.* How often, on the eve of a real revival, the minds of the people have been led away by some public entertainment in connection with the house of God, or its afterfruits withered by a series of worldly fairs and secular bids for money and the introduction of the barker and the cattle-vender into the cleansed temple of Jehovah, as in the days of Christ.

7) *The spirit of criticism and controversy is fatal to the working of the Holy Spirit.* The gentle Dove will not

remain in an atmosphere of strife. If we would cherish His power we must possess His love and frown down all wrangling gossip, evil speaking, malice, envy and public controversy in the preaching of the Word.

Sometimes a single word of criticism after an impressive service will dispel all its blessed influence upon the heart of some interested hearer and counteract the gracious work that would have resulted in the salvation of the soul.

A frivolous Christian woman was returning one night from church with her unsaved husband and laughing lightly at some of the mistakes and eccentricities of the speaker. Suddenly she felt his arm trembling; she looked in his face and his tears were falling. He gently turned to her and said: "Pray for me; I have seen myself tonight as I never did before." She suddenly awoke with an awful shudder to realize that she had been frivolously wrecking his soul's salvation and quenching the Holy Spirit.

Public controversy is as fatal to the Spirit's working as personal criticism. It is when the children of God unite at the feet of Jesus and together seek His blessing that He comes in all the fullness of His life-power.

At the Council of Nicaea it is said that a great number of grievances were sent to Constantine, the presiding officer. After the opening of the great Council, he ordered them to be gathered into the center of the large hall and then a fire kindled under them. As they went up in smoke and flame the spirit of God fell upon the assembled multitude, and they all felt that in the burning of their strifes and selfish grievances they had received the very baptism of the Holy Spirit.

The Spirit may be quenched in the hearts of our friends by unwise counsel or ungodly influence. The little child may be discouraged from seeking Christ by a worldly parent or the ignorant assumption that he or she is too young to be a Christian or too busy with studies or social enjoyments for such things.

The attractions of the world and claims and pressures of business may be interposed in the way of some seeking heart. We shall find in eternity that we put a stumbling block in our friend's way from which he fell into perdition.

Let us be very careful lest, in our willfulness and pride, we not only miss ourselves the inner chambers of the kingdom of heaven but hinder those that would enter from going in.

As we would cherish the faintest breath of life in the wretch that has been snatched from a watery grave or long to fan the expiring flame of life in a friend's body, let us be careful that we do not quench the spark of everlasting life in a human soul. Then we shall not stand at the last responsible for the murder of immortal beings and crimson with the blood of souls. "Do not put out the Spirit's fire" (1 Thessalonians 5:19).

We May Grieve the Spirit

This is a very tender expression; it suggests His gentleness and patience, grieved rather than angry with His unfaithful and distrustful children.

1. *We grieve the Holy Spirit when we doubt Him and distrust His love and promises*—just as Moses grieved Him when he struck the rock instead of gently speaking.

Many are afraid of the Holy Spirit and think Him a despot and a terror, shrinking even from His too-close approach as though He would consume us by His holiness. He wants us to love Him and come near to Him as to a gentle mother. He wants us to believe in His promises, to count Him faithful and to treat Him as One who does come to us and dwell within us.

2. *We grieve the Holy Spirit when we refuse to yield ourselves wholly to Him* and hold back from entire abandonment and surrender, or when, having so surrendered ourselves, we shrink back from His actual leading and refuse to meet the tests He brings and lie upon the wheel in stillness while He molds the clay.

He is grieved at our willfulness, rebellion and resistance. He knows we are losing a blessing and that we must again go through the same discipline if we are to have our blessings from Him.

He sees in us the spirit of distrust and unbelief, and He feels wounded and slighted by our shrinking.

3. *We grieve the Holy Spirit when we fail to enter into the fullness of His grace and receive the Lord Jesus Christ as our complete Savior.*

He has not written one word that we dare allow

to become useless. It is an insult to His wisdom and love to treat the higher visions of His grace as if they were not binding upon our life.

We should fully honor Him, press forward into all His will and feel that we owe to Him as well as ourselves that we should lose nothing of all that He has achieved, to come short of entering into His rest.

How many of His children are grieving Him as a mother would be grieved if, after having at great cost and toil provided bountifully for her children, they should refuse her bounty or despise her rich provision!

We grieve the Holy Spirit when we fail to heed His voice. He is constantly calling upon us to listen; He never speaks in vain, nor can we ever afford to miss the slightest whisper. When, therefore, we fail to listen and dash along with heedless impulsiveness, He is deeply grieved and has to call in the loud and painful tones of trial and chastening.

How He mourns for His ancient people for their refusing to listen to His loving voice: "If only you had paid attention to my commands, your peace would have been like a river, your righteousness like the waves of the sea" (Isaiah 48:18).

We grieve the Holy Spirit when, having heard, we presume to disobey His voice. This is very serious and full of terrible danger. It is an awful thing willfully to neglect or defy the distinct command of the Holy Spirit. We cannot do it without losing the sense of His presence and being conscious that He has withdrawn the manifestation of His love, until we deeply and penitently recognize our sin and step into the path of obedience where we separated from His companionship.

6) *We grieve the Holy Spirit when we have a divided heart or cherish any idols in our affections which separate our supreme love from Christ.* There is a remarkable passage in the book of James which declares that "the spirit he caused to live in us envies intensely" (James 4:5, marginal reading), and in the same connection it is added, "You adulterous people, don't you know that friendship with the world is hatred toward God?" (James 4:4), that is, a heart set upon earthly things is guilty of spiritual adultery. The Holy Spirit looks upon it with jealous love and is grieved and insulted by the dishonor done to our divine husband by our unfaithful affections.

7) *We grieve the Holy Spirit whenever we neglect, pervert or dishonor the Holy Scriptures.* This is His Word, and not one utterance or one jot shall fall to the ground. How we grieve Him when we explain away its precious promises and make of no effect its exact commands; and how He loves the heart that feeds upon the truth and honors the Bible in its least promise and command.

8) *We grieve the Holy Spirit exceedingly when we dishonor Jesus or let anything separate us from Him, cloud our conception of Him or interrupt our devotion to Him.* He is jealous for the honor of Christ. Therefore, whenever self or any human being comes between us and Christ, when the glory of the Master is obscured by the glory of the servant, when even truth or work becomes more distinct than Christ

Himself, the Holy Spirit is grieved. He is pleased, however, when we exalt the Savior and give Him all the glory.

9   *The Holy Spirit is grieved when we ignore Him.* He longs after our love and trust.

10   *The Holy Spirit is especially grieved by a spirit of bitterness toward any human being,* and therefore Paul says, "Get rid of all bitterness, rage and anger, brawling and slander, along with every form of malice" (Ephesians 4:31). "And do not grieve the Holy Spirit of God, with whom you were sealed for the day of redemption" (4:30).

III. We May Resist the Holy Spirit

This has special reference to the attitude of the unbeliever, with whom the Holy Spirit is striving with a view to convict him of sin and lead him to the Savior.

1)   *The sinner resists the Holy Spirit when he tries to shake off religious impressions.* This may be done in many ways. Sometimes the soul, under the Spirit's striving, tries to quench its impressions in pleasure, excitement or business. Sometimes it treats them as nervous depression, low spirits or ill health and seeks a remedy in change of scene or thought. Very often it resorts to light reading, worldly amusements, frivolous society—perhaps indulgence in sin. The devil always has plenty of auxiliaries to suggest distracting thoughts and help to dispel the sacred influences that God is gathering around the heart.

Very often it will become provoked and offended with some acts on the part of Christians, sometimes perhaps connected with the religious services, and will resolve to give up attending or find some petty excuse for getting out of the way of the influences that are troubling it. All these efforts to escape are only stronger evidence of the Spirit's striving, and He patiently and lovingly continues to press the arrow still more keenly into the wounded heart until it is laid prostrate at the feet of love.

2) *The sinner resists the influences of the Holy Spirit in leading him to conviction of sin.* It is not enough to awaken concern in the soul, and even alarm— there must be a distinct working of scriptural conviction in order to secure lasting peace and sound conversion. The Holy Spirit has promised to convict the world of sin. He does this by bringing before the conscience the memory of actual transgressions, the recollection of any forgotten sins, the iniquities of youth and childhood, the secret sins known to God only, the aggravations of sin, the warnings and light against which it has been committed and the love that has been resisted. He will bring up as well the threatenings of the divine law, the unchangeable holiness of the divine character, the tremendous sentence against all iniquity, the deep inward consciousness of guilt, the still more terrible sense of the wickedness of the sinner's heart, the hopeless depravity, the consciousness of willfulness and unbelief, the dreadful fear of its hopelessness and the seeming impossibility of its salvation.

Thus the Great Advocate sets in array our transgressions until the heart seeks some escape from itself. Satan is then ready to suggest a thousand excuses, palliations and false hopes, through which the guilty spirit seeks to evade the force of its conviction.

It thinks of the faults of others and plausible reasons that it is no worse than they. It eagerly seizes upon the inconsistencies of Christians and tries to excuse itself by their failure. It recalls its own miserable attempts at goodness and tries to find some comfort in its own righteousness. It seeks false refuge in the mercy of God and eagerly tries to persuade itself that the picture of Christ's anger against sin and the stories of judgment and perdition are fictions of obsolete theology.

It says, "peace, peace," when there is no peace, and attempts to heal its hurt, resisting with all its might the blessed Spirit, who wounds only that He may heal.

Happy are those who fail in the foolish attempt, and in whose hearts the arrows of the King are so sharp and keen that the wound can never be staunched except by the blood of Calvary.

The sinner resists the work of the Holy Spirit in leading him to a decision.

Even after he has been driven from his previous refuges, awakened to his profound concern, thoroughly convicted of his sin and fully admits the claims of religion and the justness of his condemnation, he seeks another door of escape in procrastination.

Perhaps he argues that he does not feel strongly enough, that he wants a deeper conviction, more light, a little more deliberate consideration, perhaps a little more time to alter his circumstances and change his life. But really what he is pleading for is a reprieve for his sinful heart, a little longer in the indulgence of his self-will and disobedience to the gospel.

And his course is just as dangerous and just as truly a rejection of Christ as if he did it deliberately and directly, while at the same time it has the self-deceiving aspect of being a sort of yielding, at least a nominal consent, to all the pleadings of the Holy Spirit.

He is resisting the Spirit, and his tomorrow often means, as the eyes of heaven read, "*Never.*"

4)   *The sinner resists the Holy Spirit in His gracious attempts to convict the soul of righteousness and lead it to believe on the Son of God.*

The Spirit's object is not merely to produce concern, alarm and even the profoundest repentance, but the ultimate goal of all His gracious movements is the acceptance of Jesus and the assurance of His forgiveness and salvation.

It is here that Satan and self-will fight their hardest battle. The soul will consent to live a better life, will be willing to weep and mourn, will do anything rather than accept the very gift of salvation and believe the naked Word of God—that its sins are forgiven for His name's sake and that it is accepted in Jesus Christ, as He is accepted.

How desperately it fights against this simple

act, clothing its unbelief in the guise of humility and modesty and thinking it presumption to dare to make such a claim!

Many souls hold back at this point for months and years and know not that in all their doubts and fears, their hard thoughts of themselves and of God, they are simply resisting the Holy Spirit, who is striving with them to lay their sins forever at the feet of Jesus and go forth into His everlasting peace.

At this point the resisting soul is led by this great enemy to erect a whole line of false refuges and run under their cover instead of fleeing for refuge directly to the hope set before it in the gospel.

One of these refuges is outward reformation of life. The sinner will do better, take the pledge, turn over a new leaf, make large promises and comfort his soul with the flattering conviction that he is a changed man, while in reality he has the same evil heart, and it will produce the same fruits when the mere effort of will has spent itself.

Another refuge of lies is a religious profession. He will get confirmed or join the church and begin a life of formalism. Perhaps he will give something to the cause of Christ and even attempt some Christian work, but he is only a whited Pharisee, and within the sepulcher are dead men's bones and all uncleanliness. And he will find before long that his old heart still has the same loves and hates, yet he has effectually suppressed the voice of the Spirit.

He meets every fear and conviction with the consciousness of his religious profession, and he will even go to the gates of the judgment hall saying, "We ate and drank with you, and you taught in our streets" (Luke 13:26), but He will "tell them plainly, 'I never knew you' " (Matthew 7:23).

Poor Ignorance, in *Pilgrim's Progress*, went up to the very gates of heaven with an easy conscience; every conviction had been stifled by his shallow professions and imagined works of self-righteousness. And so multitudes have escaped the pain of an evil conscience and the Spirit's striving to find it turn in the hour of judgment into the remorseful horror of eternal condemnation.

And so we might speak of almost countless other false refuges, all of which have the effect of quieting the troubled heart but not saving the soul. They are like sandbags thrown up in the outworks of our souls, in which the arrows of the Lord are lost or muffled but which are no protection from the armies of destruction.

It is possible for the soul to resist the Holy Spirit openly, directly, willfully and presumptuously until it drives Him from its door and commits the fatal sin of willfully rejecting the offered Savior in the full light of the Holy Spirit's revealing, and perhaps with the full consciousness that it is defiantly refusing God.

There is such a thing referred to in Scriptures: "If you resist and rebel, you will be devoured" (Isaiah 1:20); "[Y]ou rejected me when I called" (Proverbs 1:24).

If we deliberately keep on sinning after we have received the knowledge of the truth, no sacrifice for sins is left, but only a fearful expectation of judgment and of raging fire that will consume the enemies of God. Anyone who rejected the law of Moses died without mercy on the testimony of two or three witnesses. How much more severely do you think a man deserves to be punished who has trampled the Son of God under foot, who has treated as an unholy thing the blood of the covenant that sanctified him, and who has insulted the Spirit of grace? For we know him who said, "It is mine to avenge; I will repay," and again, "The Lord will judge his people." It is a dreadful thing to fall into the hands of the living God. (Hebrews 10:26-31)

The blasphemy of the Pharisees against the Holy Spirit seems to have consisted in rejecting Jesus after they had sufficient light to know that He was the Son of God.

It was, therefore, not only the rejection of Jesus, but the deliberate rejection of the Holy Spirit and His witness to Jesus when they knew it to be His witness.

Essentially, therefore, it is the same sin as any soul may now commit, when in the full light of God and conscious that He has directly called it to accept the Savior, it defiantly refuses.

The effect of such an act may be, and perhaps

usually is, the withdrawal of the Spirit from the soul until it is left, past feeling, to a hardened heart, and a doom on which the voice of divine appeal and the light of mercy will never fall again. This is, perhaps, what is meant by the blasphemy against the Holy Spirit which never finds forgiveness.

Let no one think he has committed this sin if still in the heart there is a willingness to yield to God and accept the Savior. If there is even a fear that any reader may have committed this sin, and a great longing that it may not be so, be very glad. Yield this moment even to His faint touch of heavenly influence, lest it should be withdrawn and the soul be left under the sad sentence—"Ephraim is joined to idols; leave him alone!" (Hosea 4:17).

The good Payson once said to his young friend who had spoken of a slight religious influence and wondered if it was enough to act upon:

> A little cord has dropped from heaven, so fine that you can scarcely feel it or perceive it; it just touches your shoulder for a moment. Dear friend, grasp it quickly, for it fastens to the throne of God, and it is for you perhaps the last strand of saving mercy. Grasp it and never let it go, and it will grow into a cable of strength that will anchor you to the skies and keep your precious soul unto everlasting life.

Let us be fearful and careful that we do not sin against the Holy Spirit by quenching the Spirit,

by grieving the Holy One, by resisting our best
Friend or by blaspheming His mighty name.

Books by A.B. Simpson

The Best of A.B. Simpson
    (compiled by Keith M. Bailey)
The Christ in the Bible Commentary—Six Volumes
Christ in the Tabernacle
Christ in You
The Christ of the Forty Days
The Cross of Christ
Danger Lines in the Deeper Life
Days of Heaven on Earth (devotional)
Divine Emblems
The Fourfold Gospel
The Gospel of Healing
The Holy Spirit—Power From on High
In Step with the Spirit
The Land of Promise
        (commentary on the Song of Songs)
A Larger Christian Life
The Life of Prayer
The Lord for the Body
Loving as Jesus Loves
Missionary Messages
The Names of Jesus
Portraits of the Spirit-filled Personality
Practical Christianity
Seeing the Invisible
Serving the King
The Spirit-filled Church in Action
The Supernatural
Walking in Love
When God Steps In

When the Comforter Came
Wholly Sanctified
The Word Made Flesh
    (commentary on the Gospel of John)

Booklets by A.B. Simpson

A.W. Tozer and A.B. Simpson on Spiritual Warfare
Called to Serve at Home
Christ Our Sanctifier: Reflections on the Deeper Life
Gifts and Grace
Hard Places: Stepping Stones to Spiritual Growth
Higher and Deeper: A Roadmap for Christian Maturity
Himself
Is Life Worth Living? A Study in Ecclesiastes
Paul: Ideal Man, Model Missionary
Thirty-One Kings: Victory Over Self
Women in Ministry

Books about A.B. Simpson

All for Jesus (History of The Christian and
    Missionary Alliance), by Robert Niklaus et al
*The Baptism of the Holy Spirit: The Views of A.B.
    Simpson and His Contemporaries*, by Richard
    Gilbertson
The Birth of a Vision, edited by David F. Hartzfeld
    and Charles Nienkirchen
*Body and Soul: Evangelism and the Social Concern of
    A.B. Simpson*, by Daniel J. Evearitt